Publisher's Message for
SIR JOHN'S ECHO

To shed light on today's cultural, social, economic, and political issues that are shaping our future as Canadians, Dundurn's **Point of View Books** offer readers the informed opinions of knowledgeable individuals.

Whatever the topic, the author of a **Point of View** book is someone we've invited to address a vital topic because their front-line experience, arising from personal immersion in the issue, gives readers an engaging perspective, even though a reader may not ultimately reach all the same conclusions as the author.

Our publishing house is committed to framing the hard choices facing Canadians in a way that will spur democratic debate in our country. For over forty years, Dundurn has been "defining Canada for Canadians." Now our **Point of View Books**, under the direction of general editor J. Patrick Boyer, take us a further step on this journey of national discovery.

Each author of a **Point of View** book has an important message, and a definite point of view about an issue close to their heart. Some **Point of View Books** will resemble manifestos for action, others will shed light on a crucial subject from an alternative perspective, and a few will be concise statements of a timely case needing to be clearly made.

But whatever the topic or whomever the author, all these titles will be eye-openers for Canadians, engaging issues that matter to us as citizens.

J. Kirk Howard
President
Dundurn Press

A Note from the General Editor

Historian John Boyko and I started talking at TVO's entrance as he was arriving to be interviewed by Steve Paikin about *Cold Fire: Kennedy's Northern Front*, a compelling re-examination of turning points in Canadian-American relations when John F. Kennedy was U.S. president and John G. Diefenbaker Canada's prime minister.

I'd been impressed by Boyko's talent for extracting fresh insights from our history, skill in reconstructing events with vivacious writing, and wisdom about presenting a revisionist's perspective on our past. *Cold Fire*, his sixth book, was being critically acclaimed, as had been *Blood and Daring: How Canada Fought the American Civil War and Forged a Nation*. Before that, he'd offered us a compelling reappraisal of Canada's much misunderstood eleventh prime minister, with *Bennett: The Rebel Who Challenged and Changed a Nation*.

As his students at Lakefield College and his readers appreciate, John Boyko's artful writing and rhythmic pace bring history to life. He invests constitutional battles, court rulings, and pension plans — as well as the drama of wars, strikes, and insurrections — with coherent meaning. *Sir John's Echo* pursues a storyline anchored in John Macdonald's design for a strong national government. The author creates a context within which a decades-long tumble of seemingly disconnected events, many of them loosely grouped under the rubric "federal-provincial relations" or the loftier yet more obtuse term "constitutional negotiations," are connected in an intelligible new way, thereby assuming fresh meaning.

Dundurn's Point of View books are intended to contribute to our national dialogue about issues that affect our future. Now at Confederation's 150-year mark, this long "echo" through time gives Canadians renewed inspiration in the great results that can flow, as John Boyko shows, when we embrace constructive responsibility for our country.

J. Patrick Boyer
General Editor
Point of View Books

SIR JOHN'S ECHO

Other Point of View Titles

Irresponsible Government
by Brent Rathgeber
Foreword by Andrew Coyne

Time Bomb
by Douglas L. Bland
Foreword by Bonnie Butlin

Two Freedoms
by Hugh Segal
Foreword by Tom Axworthy

Off the Street
by W.A. Bogart
Foreword by Sukanya Pillay

Charlie Foxtrot
by Kim Richard Nossal
Foreword by Ferry de Kerckhove

SIR JOHN'S ECHO

The Voice for a Stronger Canada

JOHN BOYKO

Foreword by Lawrence Martin

DUNDURN
A J. PATRICK BOYER BOOK
TORONTO

Cover image: Courtesy of Library of Congress, colour by Mark Truelove, Canadian Colour Printer: Webcom

Library and Archives Canada Cataloguing in Publication

Boyko, John, 1957-, author
        Sir John's echo : the voice for a stronger Canada / John Boyko ; foreword by Lawrence Martin.

(Point of view)
Includes bibliographical references.
Issued in print and electronic formats.
ISBN 978-1-4597-3815-7 (softcover).--ISBN 978-1-4597-3816-4
(PDF).--ISBN 978-1-4597-3817-1 (EPUB)

        1. Macdonald, John A. (John Alexander), 1815-1891--Influence. 2. Federal-provincial relations--Canada. 3. Federal government--Canada. 4. Power (Social sciences)--Canada. I. Martin, Lawrence, 1947-, writer of foreword II. Title.

JL27.B69 2016   320.471'049   C2016-907706-3

1 2 3 4 5   21 20 19 18 17

  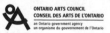

We acknowledge the support of the **Canada Council for the Arts** and the **Ontario Arts Council** for our publishing program. We also acknowledge the financial support of the **Government of Ontario**, through the **Ontario Book Publishing Tax Credit** and the **Ontario Media Development Corporation**, and the **Government of Canada**.

Care has been taken to trace the ownership of copyright material used in this book. The author and the publisher welcome any information enabling them to rectify any references or credits in subsequent editions.

— *J. Kirk Howard, President*

The publisher is not responsible for websites or their content unless they are owned by the publisher.

Printed and bound in Canada.

VISIT US AT

🌐 dundurn.com | 🐦 @dundurnpress | f dundurnpress | 📷 dundurnpress

Dundurn
3 Church Street, Suite 500
Toronto, Ontario, Canada
M5E 1M2

This book is dedicated to Kenzie and Anna,
with unreserved confidence in them and the resilient,
united country they are inheriting.

CONTENTS

FOREWORD

There is a widespread lament as we look around us today at the degree of division and political polarization in Europe and in the United States born in 2016 with the American presidential election, the success of Brexit, and the rise of Marine Le Pen in France. Faith in national governments, in national institutions, in multiculturalism has diminished at a rapid pace. White nationalism is on the move.

In Canada we find a welcome exception. We find our union as woven as it has ever been — even more unified as it celebrates its 150th anniversary than it was 50 years ago in 1967, the glowing year of the centennial when all seemed well but when Quebec secessionism was ominously finding favour.

Canada is the recipient of fulsome appraisals in the international press for bucking the trend, for moving forward in an open, progressive, multi-ethnic spirit. The divergence between what is happening here and elsewhere puts a greater premium on knowing how we reached this plateau, how the country was built, and how old battles were won. The vastness of the country makes the story all the more compelling. One need only look at the tumultuous histories of other massive territories such as Russia, China, and the United States — none of them held together with less grief than this one.

Our story can be written from various angles, but there is none more revealing than the approach taken in *Sir John's Echo*, it being the high-stakes history of the exercise of federal power versus provincial power.

The nation survived challenges to its unity from Quebec and from Alberta in more recent times, and many other challenges in preceding decades. In the past 25 years, peace has been found, the West having been "brought in" by the Stephen Harper government, the Quebec question having been put very much on the back burner after the 1995 razor-thin referendum victory of the federal side.

The template for success was set by the political savvy of John A. Macdonald. It has been his far-sighted formula, as John Boyko convincingly contends in this book, that has served as the glue of the nation. Macdonald and the other founders forged a federal state, as the author puts it, "with power resting overwhelmingly at the centre." The key to its successful evolution has resided in that centre's capacity to maintain and exercise that power in the face of myriad challenges from the provinces and, in the early decades, Great Britain.

"Sir John's Echo" weaves chronologically through the story of the interplay of the federal and provincial tug-of-war. As is seen today whenever the Liberal government wrestles with the provinces on questions of a national health-care accord, pipelines, and environmental issues, it is a never-ending narrative, one continually testing the national fibre.

In facing these challenges, the Trudeau government would do well to bear in mind the precedents. Many offer sage counsel on the art of willpower, compromise, and concession. The powers provided Ottawa at the dawn of Confederation have usually proved just sufficient enough — while engendering no shortage of bitterness in the provincial capitals — to hold sway.

Macdonald's acumen was in first recognizing, as he could well do given the astonishing carnage of the American Civil War, that the U.S. Constitution was too generous in its bestowal of powers to the states. Canada would reverse the American error "by strengthening the general government and conferring on the provincial bodies only such powers as may be required for local purposes."

As well as the Civil War, another motivator for Macdonald's strategizing was the annexation threat of the United States. This was not a time to render too many liberties to the nascent country's component parts but rather to find ways, through such ventures as the national railway, to bind them.

Macdonald's will was sometimes thwarted because Canada's Supreme Court lacked the power to render final verdicts. Decisions could be appealed to London's Judicial Committee of the Privy Council (JCPC). This became a major weapon of the provinces because the council showed bias toward their empowerment. It was several decades before the federal government was able to remove the JCPC obstacle.

Rarely was there a lengthy period in our nation's history wherein a battle with a province over the creation of a national program or national institution wasn't in progress or regress, and this book charts them all. There were the fights over conscription in two world wars, the provincial warring over the Balfour Report and the ensuing Statute of

Westminster, the Bennett government's giving birth to the Bank of Canada, and the provincial opposition to the creation of the Royal Canadian Mounted Police.

There was the provincial resistance to so many steps in the advent of the social welfare state — one example being the fight over the national health-care plan first taken up at the federal level by John Diefenbaker. There was the provincial pushback against national public radio, Trans-Canada Air Lines, and the St. Lawrence Seaway.

And major fights were still to come. They included the warring over the National Energy Plan, the 1980 referendum, and the patriation of the Constitution along with the creation of the Charter of Rights and Freedoms. Then came the fireworks over the Meech Lake Accord, and with its defeat, the repudiation of the Charlottetown Accord, both of which would have undone a good deal of Sir John's work but instead served as catalysts for the 1995 referendum.

The Conservative Party, especially in more recent decades, was the champion of provincial rights. Joe Clark's vision was of Canada as a community of communities. Brian Mulroney's accords sought to reduce federal powers. Stephen Harper's philosophy leaned more toward decentralization. He declined to hold first ministers' conferences for fear they would create discord with the provinces. Indeed, many conferences did over the years, but they were important to the nation-building process.

The capacity of Ottawa to maintain and in some cases enhance powers owed itself in many cases to happenstance. The two world wars brought on a rally-around-the-flag effect, a necessity for provincial leaders to put aside their parochial priorities and abide by the national will. Powers greatly accrued to Ottawa. The Second World War saw the creation of 28 Crown corporations. Ontario Premier Mitch Hepburn vigorously opposed the pace of Prime Minister William Lyon Mackenzie King's war effort, having a resolution passed through his legislature to that effect. King used the Queen's Park opposition to trigger an election, which he won handily.

The prime ministers were not, by a long shot, always right in forcing the hand of the premiers. Few better examples were evident than at the outset of the Great Depression when provincial demands piled up for Ottawa's social assistance. King paid little heed, holding to the line that the government's job was to stay out of the way and let the market do the job. He became an egregious partisan on the matter, saying that he might be prepared to help some Liberal premiers on questions of unemployment, "but I would not give a single cent to any Tory government … I would not give them a five-cent piece." An uproar ensued. He soon called the country to the polls. His Liberals were thrashed.

The Macdonald vision never received a greater endorsement than the one it was given by the people. That happened in the 1992 Charlottetown referendum. Virtually all the elites in the country — the premiers, the federal parties, the business community, the academic community, the journalistic community — agreed on the advisability of this decentralizing pact and advocated for it. But average Canadians voted it down in firm fashion. The echo of Sir John still resonated.

Stephen Harper's government had no use for national programs. It killed the Kelowna Accord and a national daycare plan. It killed the long-form census. An architect of the Reform Party, Harper was no fan of the Macdonald vision. At one point, before coming to power in Ottawa, he advocated building a firewall against Ottawa around Alberta. His small federal government vision was rejected in the election of 2015. With an activist agenda, with plans for the renewal of federal-provincial conferences and the renewal of national programs, Justin Trudeau came to power with a majority government.

"It was evidence," writes John Boyko, that the Macdonald vision of the country "had survived the decentralizing provincial phoenix that had risen in Brian Mulroney's shadow and Stephen Harper's moment." The original vision held, as it always had.

John Boyko's book illuminates with perceptive precision the dynamic that made Canada work. It is a striking contribution to the understanding of our history.

Lawrence Martin, *a public affairs columnist for the* Globe and Mail, *where he served as correspondent in Washington, D.C., Moscow, Montreal, and Ottawa, is the author of 10 books on Canadian history, politics, and sports.*

A strong and dominant national feeling is not a luxury in Canada.… Without it this country could not exist.

— William Lyon Mackenzie King

INTRODUCTION:
THE QUESTION

Families were split. Friendships ended. There were workplace arguments and businesses lost customers. Neighbours who had gotten on well for years found themselves in finger-wagging spats. Canadians in big cities and little towns gathered in stuffy church basements and hot school gyms to discuss and debate. Many meetings heard shouts and chants as tempers flared. A question about the state was tearing up the nation.

It was all about power. Power divides talk and action. Whether in the course of our busy lives we take time to think about it, political power touches us all. It affects the lives of our children and will influence theirs. Power, of course, confers the ability to influence people to do what they might not otherwise do. Positively expressed, state power offers a vehicle through which people are encouraged and enabled to act collectively for the common good. Power matters, and so it matters who has it.

Through that tough summer and fall of 1992, Canadians were preparing to vote in a national referendum to determine whether the power to shape their country and therefore influence their lives and family's futures should lie primarily with the government in Ottawa or be diffused to the provinces and territories. We were being asked to consider who speaks for us and for our country. Revolutions have been fought over such questions. The question has led to marches, riots, and bloody *coups d'état*. Whether power should rest with the national or state governments was at the core of the American Civil War that took more than 600,000 lives.

But we're Canadians. Where others might reach for a gun, we go for a gavel. While our history is spattered with blood-spilling spasms, the 1992 referendum campaign saw debates, but no violence. There were gatherings, but no tear gas. The political, business, and media elites were united in their opinion that the federal government should be weakened and then shocked when so many disobedient Canadians appeared to believe otherwise. They were aghast when the vote revealed that a majority of Canadians had said no to their idea and no to them. It was quite a *civil* civil war.

The no the populace delivered to the leaders of the country was a yes to its founders. Over a century and a quarter before, in 1864, British North American colonial representatives had also taken to meeting rooms rather than battlefields. Led by John A. Macdonald, they responded to American threats of invasion, British threats of desertion, and economic threats of bankruptcy by creating a country from chaos. The founders forged a federal state with power resting overwhelmingly at the centre. The provinces would be glorified municipalities while the federal government would speak for Canada.*

As soon as the fireworks announcing the country's birth in July 1867 cooled, the push-and-pull power struggles between the federal and provincial governments sparked to life. The fights continued through wars, depressions, and periods of dizzying prosperity. It was that old fight that had been foisted upon us again in 1992.

We were right to reject the elites then and support Sir John. We were right to exclaim, as he did, that our federal government is a positive force that helps define and then enhance the greater good, and so it needs, deserves, and has earned sufficient power to unite, build, and speak for Canada. Throughout Canada's tumultuous history, it is the federal government that has always led acts of nation building, whether through the construction of railways, highways, and seaways or the signing of treaties, trade deals, and charters. Far too often, parochial provincial premiers sought to stymie or sabotage those efforts. At the same time, premiers have been quick to call on the federal government for help in times of economic, political, or natural crisis. As Sir John intended, the federal government is Canada's builder, first responder, and voice. Its power is legitimate and essential.

This is not to say that premiers are not patriots and provinces don't matter. Of course they are and of course they do. Provincial governments are an important element of the

---

* Words are funny in that their meaning keeps changing. Consider that something great can be both "hot" and "cool." For our more immediate purposes, consider that a federal system refers to a state with two levels of government, and yet we call our national government "the" federal government. The word is not really right, but it has fallen into common usage and so during our visit together over the following pages, let's call that government in Ottawa representing us all the Canadian, or national, or federal government — or even just Ottawa.

Canadian state and contribute mightily to our lives. Provincial governments have always done as the founders hoped they would: tended to local matters while sometimes acting as incubators for ideas that occasionally become national programs. Saskatchewan's public health-care initiative is one example of this, and Ontario's abandoning coal to tackle climate change is another. Provincial co-operation with the federal government has been an essential element in the creation and maintenance of pan-Canadian endeavours that have helped express our citizenship.

The point is not patriotism, but perspective. Each premier, regardless of party, quite properly works for what is best for his or her province. A rare few have undertaken their primary job while risking unpopularity at home to stand boldly for the national interest. Every prime minister, on the other hand, is called to consider not what is best for a particular province, or for his or her party, pension, or personal ambition, but for all of Canada and for all Canadians. In the struggle for the power to build, address emergencies, and speak for the country as a whole, prime ministers have fought, cajoled, and allied with premiers and always with perspective trumping party.

Canada is a conversation. Every election, every new law, every audacious public initiative that swells our chests, or staggering crisis that draws our tears, is another measure of that conversation. And when we're talking, we're always talking about power. So let's talk. Let's consider the idea that while some national leaders have made tragic and bone-headed decisions, that as a nation builder and first responder, the federal government is a force for good. Let's explore the messy but fascinating story of our over 150-year national conversation with the idea that Canada is at its best when the power Sir John gave the federal government is used to act and speak for Canada — and the idea that we go off the rails when we distort that vision. As we explore the characters and calamities that made us, let's see if we become a little more willing to embrace Sir John's vision and consider ourselves not narrowly as of a particular province, but more broadly as Canadians, stronger and richer in the complexity of our shared national citizenship.

1

THE FOUNDERS' INTENTIONS

John A. Macdonald was gone. He had missed nearly a week in the pre-Confederation Canadian legislature. A drunk and dishevelled Macdonald yawned open his rooming house door and squinted through watery eyes at a young man who demanded his immediate return to duties. Macdonald mumbled that if the governor general was responsible for the message then he could go to hell, but if the gentleman was there at his own behest, then he could take the trip himself. The door slammed. The tale is either endearing or disturbing.

Sir John is tough to love, but tougher to hate. The lanky man with the high forehead, wiry and unruly hair, prominent nose, and dancing eyes was a rogue, but he was our rogue. He was a charmer and a ruthless operator. Macdonald can be applauded for efforts to afford more rights for women and for promoting better understanding between the French and English, but he should also be condemned for racist attitudes and policies toward Chinese workers and Aboriginal nations. A scoundrel and a scamp, Macdonald was a hail-fellow-well-met, a loyal friend, and a fierce enemy. He was Canada's indispensable man because nation building is both mechanical and organic and so demands both architects and gardeners. Structures might be put in place, but as with any venture involving unpredictable and often irrational human beings, it is slow growth and adjustment to changing conditions that test and either strengthen those structures or tear them asunder. Fortunately, at its birth and through early, perilous years, Canada enjoyed the perfect marriage of man and moment. Sir John A. Macdonald was Canada's architect and gardener, with the personality, skills, and vision to be expert at both.

In the fall of 1864, Macdonald was in a small, high-ceilinged, ornate room in Charlottetown. He knew, as did the other delegates from the British North American colonies of Canada (Quebec and Ontario), Nova Scotia, New Brunswick, and Prince Edward Island, that they were in trouble. The Americans had been butchering themselves in a civil war for three years. Confederate spies openly operated from Toronto and Montreal, and unscrupulous crimpers were tricking and even kidnapping young men to become Union soldiers. American generals, newspapers, and powerful politicians were advocating an invasion that would quickly overwhelm the thin red line of British soldiers and undertrained colonial militia. Meanwhile, British politicians were falling under the sway of those demanding an end to military and financial support for their expensive and troublesome colonies. Britain had withdrawn from a trade agreement that had greatly benefitted the British North American colonies and the United States had pledged to do the same, with both actions contributing to economic hardship. Beyond all of that, the political structures that had been created in response to disquiet in the Maritimes and rebellions in Upper and Lower Canada had proven themselves dysfunctional and clearly unequal to the challenges of the day. In the face of economic, political, and military hazards, the colonial governments were broken and broke.

After just a few hours of discussion, the Charlottetown delegates agreed that to save themselves they needed to create themselves. Unification was the answer. The question was how. There were two models upon which they could base their new country. The British parliamentary system of government was most appealing to the loyal British subjects around the big table. However, Quebec delegates agreed with those from the Maritimes that, unlike Britain, a new Canada needed not just a central government but a federal system to allow sub-national governments to protect local rights and identities. The essential question quickly became how much power should be placed with the central government and how much should be apportioned to the provinces. It is the question that has shaped our history and haunts us still.

On this matter, the United States offered a compelling and alarmingly negative example. While the American Constitution was brilliant in its conception, the booming Union and Confederate cannons, shattered cities, and armies-worth of mourning widows demonstrated its appalling failure in practice. Sir John and others said the American Constitution's problem and the main reason the United States was currently eating its young was that too much power had been located in the sub-national state governments.

Macdonald explained to Confederation delegates that he admired the U.S. Constitution and respected the work and vision of its framers. However, he observed, "The dangers that have arisen from this system will be avoided if we can agree upon a strong central government — a great central legislature — a constitution for a Union which will have all the rights of sovereignty except those that are given to the local governments. Then we shall have taken a great step in advance of the American Republic."[1] He repeated the point when the conference moved to cool and rainy Quebec City. Perched in grand rooms offering spectacular views of the thundering St. Lawrence, delegates drew closer to hammering out the new Constitution's details. Canada would reverse the "primary error" of the United States, Macdonald said, "by strengthening the general government and conferring on the provincial bodies only such powers as may be required for local purposes."[2]

The Charlottetown and Quebec City conferences were spectacular successes. Despite the fact that Newfoundland and, ironically, Prince Edward Island decided not to join, the delegates had undertaken a peaceful, respectful state-building project like few in the world had ever done. No armies marched. No shots were fired. No one died or, for that matter, was threatened, beaten up, or arrested. We began our national conversation by talking ourselves into a country.

As the process moved to the ratification stage, Macdonald repeatedly used the American example to remind the wavering and unconvinced of his reason for locating so much power with the federal government. In a speech to the Canadian legislature, he said:

> The American Constitution … commenced, in fact, at the wrong end. They declared by their constitution that each state was a sovereignty in

itself, and that all the powers incident to a sovereignty belonged to each state, except those powers which, by the constitution, were confirmed upon the General Government and Congress. Here we have adopted a different system. We have strengthened the General Government. We have given the General Legislature all the great subjects of legislation.[3]

When Queen Victoria signed the British North America Act in 1867, the provinces were as Macdonald, George-Étienne Cartier, Alexander Galt, George Brown, Charles Tupper, Samuel Tilley, and the other founders intended. They were akin to municipalities. Section 92 of the new Constitution ceded only 16 powers to the four original provinces. They included education; the regulation of hospitals, asylums, and charities; the issuing of shop, saloon, tavern, and auctioneer licences; the solemnization of marriage, as well as the protection of property and civil rights; the administration of justice; the management of public lands, including the sale of wood and timber; and, finally, direct taxation within each province. The only addition was that Section 95 rendered agriculture and immigration as concurrent or shared powers in which the federal and provincial governments would co-operate. It is interesting that while the primary reason Cartier and French-speaking Quebecers demanded a federal system was to protect their language and religion, Section 92 was silent on both.

Among the powers allocated to the federal government in Section 91 were the militia, military, and naval service; defence; navigation and shipping; the postal service; criminal law; marriage and divorce; immigration; and the responsibility for Aboriginals and Aboriginal land. The federal government's financial powers were immense. They included responsibility for currency and coinage, banking, bankruptcy and insolvency, trade and commerce, public debt and property, and in a phrase that was potent in its ambiguity, "the raising of money by any mode or system of taxation." By giving the federal government the power to levy direct and indirect taxes and limiting provinces to collecting only direct taxes, the federal government was rendered fiscally powerful and the provinces set up to be poor cousins.

The lists made clear where the fiscal and legislative power would lie, but there was even more. In the United States, to balance legislative representation between big and little states, it was decided to base the House of Representatives on representation by population but to allocate two seats per state in the Senate. In 1867, and until 1913, state legislatures appointed senators. Macdonald and his centralist colleagues determined that House of Commons members would be elected through representation by population. As in the United States and Britain, the upper house would be filled by appointment. However, unlike in the United States, the federal government, really the prime minister, would do the appointing and the Senate would reflect not provinces but regions.

There was more. Provincial premiers were constitutionally bound to work with lieutenant governors, who were appointed by the monarch but became federal government appointees in practice. The BNA Act gave lieutenant governors reserve power. With this power, rather than being obliged to sign all provincial bills into law, lieutenant governors could send questionable ones to the federal government for consideration. Provincial bills could then be killed through interminable delay. Sections 55 and 56 also gave the federal government the power of disallowance. That is, it could deem any provincial law in contradiction of the best interests of the county, and even if legally passed by a provincial legislature and signed by a lieutenant governor, simply rip it up.

Also in Section 92 was the declaratory power that gave the federal government the right, whenever it determined that a particular public work would benefit Canada as a whole, to take control of a project and land, regardless of the provincial government's opinion or constitutional power over the matter.

Finally, the federal government was given residuary power. While the wording of this portion of the Constitution was infuriatingly vague, its intention was clear: anything that fell between the constitutional cracks or that came up later that the Constitution did not specifically address (who would regulate the Internet or airports, for example) would automatically go to the federal government.

Sir John was a late convert to the Confederation idea. He lent support only when it had become politically expedient as well as the best way forward. Even then, he had opposed a federal state, arguing instead for a more efficient and more British style of legislative union with no sub-national governments. He later relented when Quebec's George-Étienne Cartier and Ontario's George Brown made federalism a condition of their support. It is clear that with the new country's Constitution, much of which was written in his hand, Macdonald had won the next best thing to a legislative union. The provinces were as weak as they could be while still having any power at all.

In 1867, Canada was a baby country. Much of what would later define its sovereignty, such as control of foreign policy, the power to conduct its own judicial reviews, treaty-making powers, and the ability to amend its Constitution, still lay with London. While the United States was still focused on recovering from the Civil War and fighting its Indian Wars, it remained a threat. Most of the country's leaders believed in Manifest Destiny, a doctrine based on the notion that it was not just right but inevitable that all of North America would some-day become the United States. The U.S. purchase of Alaska in the same year as Confederation was justified to congressional skeptics as part of that grand strategy that would someday make Canada American and chase Britain from the continent.

While operating within British restraints and with an eye to the Americans, Macdonald moved his vision of a transcon-tinental country forward while also dealing with troublesome provinces. An early threat came from Nova Scotia. Its first post-Confederation elections saw 18 of 19 federal seats and 34 of 36 provincial seats won by anti-Confederation candidates. It appeared that the province was heading out of Canada as the southern states had so recently left the United States. Losing Nova Scotia would have robbed Canada of its Atlantic border and possibly shattered the new country, leaving Washington to pick up the pieces.

The leader of the anti-Confederation Nova Scotians, and the province's new premier, was Joseph Howe, the brilliant scholar, newspaperman, and political gadfly. His success at the polls did not lead to any success with his anti-Confederation crusade, however. Howe received a cold reception in London, where he unsuccessfully lobbied British leaders to let his people go. He returned to a series of warm gestures from Macdonald.

Howe was offered a seat on the Railway Commission and a hand in naming some other federal government appointments. Then the province was given a greater annual subsidy than the Confederation deal had pledged. Finally, Howe left Halifax to accept a seat in Macdonald's cabinet. The secessionist movement slowly died away. It was quite appropriate that once when checking into a hotel, Macdonald had recorded his occupation as cabinetmaker.

Threats from the provinces continued, and in addressing them Macdonald continued to be more pragmatic than doctrinaire. In his government's first six years, he disallowed only five provincial laws: two from Nova Scotia, two from Quebec, and one from Ontario. In each case, the laws were clearly ultra vires — that is, beyond the province's constitutional jurisdiction. He understood that the provinces were useful in addressing local matters, and with respect to Quebec, in handling what at the time were still called "racial" problems between the French and English.

He wrote to the *Montreal Gazette* in 1868: "The questions of conflict of jurisdiction have pretty nearly all developed themselves, and must ere long be settled ... they should be approached in a statesman like spirit, and not in a vain attempt on the part of either of the Local or Dominion Statesmen, to gain a victory."[4]

It was a nice thought, but he was too experienced and smart to really believe it, for he knew better than most that power never sleeps. In politics, power is a zero-sum game. The provinces were active players in attempts to win power for themselves even if it meant sabotaging nation-building efforts and turning Canada from development along the centralist lines that the country's founders intended. The often simultaneous two-front battles were political and legal. The first and most consequential of those efforts came not from Quebec and the Maritimes, both of which had most vociferously demanded a federal state in the first place, but from Ontario.

A young Oliver Mowat had clerked in Macdonald's Kingston law firm. He became a Liberal and a thorn in his former mentor's side. In 1861, Mowat's hectoring in the legislature crossed the line and Macdonald crossed the aisle. He grabbed the shorter man's lapels, yanked him from the floor, and yelled, "You damned pup! I'll slap your chops." Shocked members pulled Macdonald away before he could make good on his threat. Macdonald neutered Mowat by appointing him to the Court of the Chancery, but in 1872 he was back, this time as Ontario's premier.

The year after Mowat won his office, Macdonald lost his due to a scandal involving a railway executive stuffing Conservative Party coffers. Liberal Prime Minister Alexander Mackenzie lacked Macdonald's political acumen and statesman's vision, but he understood the centralist Constitution. In his five years as prime minister, he worked to protect the federal government's power and disallowed 18 provincial laws. Meanwhile, Mowat built an Ontario dynasty based partly on filling every public service job in the province with a Liberal. Mowat was channelling American President Andrew Jackson, who had advised his secretary of war, "If you have a job in your department that can't be done by a Democrat, then abolish the job."

With his back safe and base stable, Mowat moved to secure his vision of a more decentralized Canada by creating a more sovereign Ontario. The competing visions of Canada came to a head over the headwaters of Ontario's Mississippi River, southwest of Ottawa. Boyd, Caldwell and Company had begun floating logs down the Mississippi, but Peter McLaren said he had paid for the building of dams and shoreline improvements and obtained an injunction to have the company stopped. In response to the legal spat, Premier Mowat passed the 1881 Act for Protecting the Public Interest in Rivers, Streams, and Creeks. It allowed anyone to use private improvements on waterways if the owner was properly paid. The federal Conservatives had been re-elected, and Macdonald was back as prime minister when the Mississippi mess hit his desk.

Macdonald saw Mowat's law as a brash attempt to exert and expand provincial power in a way that would weaken Canada. He disallowed it. The federal government, Sir John argued, must protect the interests of the country when local cases had national implications. If the Ontario law were allowed to stand, he said, then property rights throughout Canada would be threatened and capitalists would be less likely to invest anywhere in the country. He explained his primary principle in the House: "The autonomy of every province, the independence of every province, the independence of every Legislature, should be protected unless there is a constitutional reason against it. [However] … Sir, we are not half a dozen Provinces. We are one great Dominion."[5] Mowat tweaked the law and passed it again. Macdonald disallowed it again. Over the next three years, it was passed and disallowed again and then passed a fourth time. The case then moved from the political realm to the judicial.

The founders had debated the need for a Supreme Court to settle such matters, but could not agree on its powers or membership. Macdonald had brought forth a bill to establish a Canadian Supreme Court in 1869 and again the next year, but both were killed by provincial concerns that were ably expressed by provincial spokesmen and Quebec MPs. They echoed provincial fears that a powerful federal body could make decisions that might render infringements on their jurisdictions permanent. The proposed court was seen for what it was: Macdonald trying to create yet another instrument to model the relationship between the central and provincial governments like the one that had existed between London and the colonies.

An acceptable Supreme Court bill was finally passed in April 1875. Because the Confederation deal acknowledged the existence of one system of law in Quebec, where civil law was based on French traditions and criminal law on British common law, and another system in the other provinces, where both civil and criminal law were based on British common law, Quebec was guaranteed three justices on the court.

While the provinces remained unhappy, the Supreme Court was hardly supreme. Cases could be taken to the new Canadian court, but its decisions could be appealed to a British body based on a 15th-century idea that had been formalized in the 1830s. The Judicial Committee of the Privy Council (JCPC) was comprised of robed and wigged British Lords who gathered in London around a large circular table with one chair always reserved for but never taken by the monarch. They ruled on cases from the British Admiralty, the Church of England, and the colonies. Discussions were secret and decisions final. Canadian Supreme Court decisions could be overruled by the JCPC, and the court had to adhere to Lords' precedents. Provinces could skip right over the Supreme Court and take cases to the JCPC.

In a nod to the growing independence of some of its colonies, Britain opened JCPC membership to representatives from Canada, South Africa, and Australia in 1895. However, allowing colonial Supreme Court justices to sit at the table was inconsequential, as they were seldom able to attend and over the years made few substantive contributions to rulings. Their membership was a salve to the colonies more than a genuine recognition of sovereignty.

It was to the JCPC that the federal-provincial rivers and streams spat was taken. Under the leadership of Lord Watson, Macdonald's disallowance was disallowed.

The case reeked of consequence. From that point forward, the federal government was less able to disallow laws that were within a province's jurisdiction, even if they were deemed contrary to the national interest. Furthermore, with the case establishing the JCPC's obvious bias against the federal government's dominance, provinces were inspired to pass more laws pushing and testing the limits of their power. If stymied by the federal government, they just leaped over its head to London's Lords, who showed themselves determined to undo the BNA Act's spirit and contradict its authors' intentions.

A sure sign that the power shift was on came about the same time that Macdonald was losing his fight on the Mississippi, but this time, perhaps ironically for him, the brawl began in a bar. A Toronto tavern owner named Archibald Hodge was fined under an Ontario law forbidding his customers from playing billiards after the provincially mandated Saturday closing time of 7:00 p.m. (Toronto the Good was more than a nickname in those days!) Hodge hired a lawyer who argued that Ottawa's Temperance Act superseded the Ontario law and had no such provision. The case went all the way to the JCPC. Again siding with the provinces, the JCPC supported Ontario's right to overrule the Canadian law and apply its own.

The effects of 1883's *Hodge v. the Queen* were as staggering as anything Hodge might have served at his tavern, because the JCPC decision was predicated on the opinion that laws regarding trade and commerce were not the federal government's sole discretion. Even more important, it presented a new interpretation of the BNA Act's crucial Section 91.

The section's first part says that the federal government may "make laws for the Peace, Order, and Good Government of Canada, in relation to all matters not coming within the Classes and Subject by the Act assigned exclusively to the Legislatures of the Provinces …" This clause was followed by the already noted list of exclusive federal powers. Macdonald and the founders, in their Confederation debates, and even early JCPC decisions, made clear that the list simply contained examples of how the Peace, Order, and Good Government clause could be applied. The *Hodge v. the Queen* interpretation changed everything by separating the clause from the list. That is, the powers enumerated in the list were deemed to be not just examples of Ottawa's power, but its precise limits. The Peace, Order, and Good Government clause could only apply, the JCPC said, where there was a clear gap in the listed powers or in times of national emergency. Racking up the balls on Hodge's billiard table past closing time was perhaps important to the thirsty gamesmen, but, it argued, hardly constituted a national emergency.

The empire was striking back. With these two decisions and subsequent ones, the JCPC clearly demonstrated that it was undoing what Sir John and the founders intended in the belief that it knew what was best for Canadians. It was ignoring and contradicting Canada's prime minister, history, and current political customs. By spinning the interpretation of the Constitution, it was twisting its spirit by moving toward a more American model of strong sub-national governments and a weak centre. Lord Huldane, who presided over the JCPC from 1911 to 1928, was blunt in explaining that he and his predecessor, Lord Watson, acted to reverse Canadian wishes. In a 1923 speech to the Cambridge Law Society, Huldane said:

> At one time after the [BNA Act] was passed, the conception took hold of the Canadian Courts that what was intended was to make the Dominion the centre of the government in Canada, so that its statutes and position should be superior to the statutes and position of the Provincial Legislatures. That went so far that there arose a great fight; and as the result of a long series of decisions Lord Watson put clothing upon the bones of the Constitution, and so covered them over with living flesh that the Constitution of Canada took new form. The Provinces were recognized as of equal authority and co-ordinate with the Dominion, and a long series of decisions were given by him, which solved many problems and produced a new contentment in Canada with the Constitution they had got in 1867.[6]

Canadian Supreme Court justice and constitutional scholar Bora Laskin called Watson and Huldane the "wicked step-fathers of Confederation." Their actions reflected the advice received by a gentleman working with the JCPC who was an ex-Confederate American and strident proponent of states' rights. Their decisions also reflected the concept of Canada promoted by those like Ontario's Oliver Mowat and Edward Blake, Ontario's second premier. Blake spoke of Canada not as a unified country but a mere compact between the provinces. He often referred not to Canada's destiny but its destinies. Blake, Mowat, the Lords, and others were like Americans whose words betray attitudes when they say the United States "are" rather than the United States "is." An Ontario attorney demonstrated his understanding of the compact theory of Canada when, in a case before the JCPC, he used words that would have resonated among "are-saying" Americans and those who formed the Confederacy, but sent chills through Sir John and those struggling to build a unified country. He argued, "The provinces are virtually separate countries…. Each is a separate state."[7]

While right about the power shift, and there were many more cases that accelerated it, Lord Huldane was wrong in predicting contentment with the new reality. After all, giving someone a little of something usually generates more hunger than satiation — especially when the meal is power. With Ontario leading the way, the provinces became ravenous.

Macdonald knew how to pick his battles and chose not to fight the London Lords. Instead, he sidestepped them and the provinces and used the federal government's power and his adroit political skills to build the young country. Sir John would outmanoeuvre the legal fights that were confounding the founders' vision by using his political acumen to advance it. Two actions were essential to that effort.

The first involved saving Canada. In 1870, Macdonald had negotiated the purchase of Rupert's Land from the Hudson's Bay Company. For $1.5 million, the federal government bought what is now northern Quebec and Ontario and much of the northern Prairies, Northwest Territories, and Nunavut. It was about a third of Canada's current land mass. Aboriginal nations really owned it, but, sadly, Macdonald ignored them.

The Americans had wanted it, but Macdonald out-foxed them. The purchase, however, did not quell talk of annexation and Manifest Destiny that warmed the blood of American political elites and informed civil society conversations over mugs of beer in dusky bars and sips of sherry in private clubs.

The Americans were still upset with the actions of Britain and Canada during their 1861–65 Civil War. They sought compensation for the costs incurred due to Britain having surreptitiously provided ships to the Confederacy. Called the *Alabama* Claims, based on the name of the deadliest of the vessels, American Secretary of State Hamilton Fish told British Ambassador Edward Thornton that President Ulysses S. Grant was frustrated by a lack of progress on the file. He wanted either the $2.125 billion suggested by the chair of America's Senate Foreign Relations Committee or ownership of Canada. The sum was astronomical — consider that in 1867 the United States bought Alaska for only $7.2 million — and so the ambassador admitted that the swap was tempting. Grant confided to an aide that the seven-year reparations fight could end in five minutes if Canada was simply ceded to the United States.[8] In February 1871, a conference was convened in Washington, D.C., to settle matters. There were five Americans, including the secretary of state, four British representatives, and Macdonald.

Macdonald took the conference so seriously that he even stopped drinking. British pressure on the Canadian was even greater than that from the American delegates, but he was brilliant in his negotiating tactics and steely in his determined defence of the young country's interests and sovereignty. The British delegates insisted that Macdonald surrender to U.S. demands. Meanwhile, he even had to fight Canadian Governor General Lisgar, who took cabled reports regarding Sir John's first and fallback positions and secretly rerouted them to the British delegates in Washington.

The conference concluded with Macdonald winning a 12-year fishing-rights agreement that bolstered the Nova Scotia and New Brunswick economies and afforded an incentive for Prince Edward Island to join Confederation. Macdonald also won an end to American tariffs on a number of goods, which helped Ontario and Quebec. He also negotiated a $2.5 million British loan guarantee as compensation for the Fenian raids in which angry Irish-American nationalists had spilled over the border in doomed attempts to capture Canada and trade it for Irish independence. More important, it was agreed that the *Alabama* Claims would be settled through international arbitration with the cash-for-Canada swap off the table. Finally, and of major significance, Macdonald secured agreement that the Washington Treaty would come into effect only with the ratification of the British, American, and Canadian legislatures. For the first time, Canada was recognized as more than just a British colony. Macdonald returned to Ottawa justifiably proud of his accomplishments, for he had saved Canada in a moment of crisis and demonstrated that the federal government was the country's one and true voice. He no doubt celebrated with a tumbler or two, or perhaps three.

Sir John built upon what had been saved. In 1879, he introduced the National Policy. It engaged overlapping tactics, all seeking to make Canada bigger and richer and more secure. During the 1864 Confederation conferences, Canadian delegates had argued that one of the main benefits of the new union would be the money to be made and security to be augmented by creating a transcontinental country. It was that urge that had motivated Macdonald to purchase Rupert's Land. Now, with the Americans still worrisome, the economy still troublesome, the provinces still bothersome, and national ambitions outpacing financial capacity, Macdonald needed to exploit the newly acquired territory.

An important element of the National Policy involved the building of a railway from the Atlantic to the Pacific. The people of British Columbia had considered joining the United States. While sentimentality whispered that they should join Canada, money, not talking but swearing as it does, screamed they should become American. Saving the Confederation dream demanded bringing British Columbia into Canada and so Macdonald promised not just a wagon trail from Calgary or a rail link through the northern states but an all-Canadian train from Toronto. And he would have it in Vancouver in 10 years. It was an audacious pledge. It would be the world's longest railway, built over the world's most inhospitable real estate. Few believed it could really be done and none according to the timetable. But the promise worked, and British Columbians ignored their heads and voted with their hearts to join Canada.

Building the railway nearly bankrupted the country. It led to Macdonald losing his government in an 1873 railway-related scandal before returning five years later. It also led to Aboriginal land being taken and rights ignored and Chinese labour being ruthlessly exploited. However, with the driving of the last spike in November 1885, a visionary, albeit ruthless, prime minister had used the power that only the federal government could wield to ensure that an undeniable demonstration of Canada's sovereignty had been constructed.

The country now had the means to fill and enrich itself. Macdonald had passed the Dominion Land Act in 1872 to attract settlers to the West. A combination of factors rendered the desired flood a mere trickle. It would be a generation before domestic and global dynamics brought the deluge. Meanwhile, Macdonald instituted a second tenet of the National Policy, the erection of tariffs, to build the infant economy.

The tariffs placed on various imported goods were designed to raise money when they crossed the border but also to boost their prices so that Canadian consumers would be persuaded to purchase cheaper Canadian-made products and thereby stimulate the growth and prosperity of domestic manufacturers. At the time, tariffs made up the majority of Ottawa's revenue. The highest tariffs, critics observed, were not protective at all but blatant revenue generators slapped on many goods not even made or grown in Canada, such as chocolate, coffee, and coconuts. Macdonald made no secret of the fact that the new tariffs were partly designed to increase those earnings. He was also unapologetic when other critics noted that the new tariffs gave a preponderance of help not to all Canadians but to Toronto and Montreal business people who happened also to be strong Conservative Party supporters. He was further attacked, then and later, for the policy's helping eastern urban manufacturers while forcing western farmers to buy more expensive Canadian machinery and other goods when cheaper American products were effectively stopped at the border. Macdonald was as unmoved by all the gnashing of teeth as he was by others who berated him for not allowing the building of spur lines from the Canadian Pacific Railway (CPR) to the United States, lest they encourage more north-south rather than the east-west trade the National Policy was designed to encourage.

Despite the criticism, and while premiers were still appealing to Ottawa and the Lords for more power, Canada grew on the federal government's steel rails and behind its tariff walls. The country reoriented itself, as Sir John intended, on an east-west axis. The western provinces are the railway's children, with their growth built on what would become three transcontinental lines. To check a map of today's major cities is to see the original routes. The marketplace still ruled, with only a small amount of investment having gone to companies that would have failed without Ottawa's largess. Sir John's National Policy allowed the support and protection needed for the industry of workers, the courage of investors, the determination of pioneers, and the clever leadership of executives to combine in the building of the country.

No country's destiny is assured. All may fail. There was no guarantee that Canada would survive any longer than the many others that in the 19th century were rising and falling or that North America would not someday resemble a European hodgepodge of small countries with ever-shifting borders. By the century's end, however, despite provinces attempting to alter the founders' intentions in their squabbling for scraps of power and the JCPC forcing bifocals on the founders' vision, the federal government had led the way in seeing Canada born, saved, and afforded the means to grow.

We were still largely a country of farmers and fishers. Most people still considered themselves British more than Canadian. But too soon, the shooting of an unknown Austrian prince in an obscure Bosnian town would lead Germany to invade Belgium and result in Canadian boys leaving home to kill German boys. The Great War changed everything. It changed Canada. And it made our federal government even more important than ever.

2

THE GREAT WAR

The First World War was a stupid war fought in a stupid way for stupid reasons by incredibly courageous young men. At Ypres, in April 1915, Canadians had their first real taste of the brutality that matched 18th-century thinking with 19th-century tactics and 20th-century weapons. More than 6,500 brave men were killed, wounded, or taken prisoner. Ypres shook Canadians. The war nearly shook Canada apart.

The years leading to war had seen premiers continue to demand and the British court continue to grant more and more power to the provinces. The federal government continued to work around the distractions and impediments to build the country and respond to emergencies. After Macdonald's death in 1891, a succession of failed Conservative leaders eventually led, in 1896, to a Liberal victory and Wilfrid Laurier became prime minister. He was a brilliant political strategist and wily tactician whose actions again illustrated the federal government's essential and progressive power.

Macdonald's railway had led to enormous growth but also to rebellions in Manitoba and Saskatchewan, the robbing of Aboriginal land, and the shameful mistreatment of Aboriginal peoples. It also left Canada with a problem. The Prairies were now Canada's but needed more people.

The 1872 Dominion Land Act legislated Ottawa's power over immigration rules and the distribution of land. A number of schemes had been tried by Macdonald to attract settlement, and many people had come, but not in the necessary numbers. Laurier inherited a better domestic and global economy, put a better minister in charge, and approved a better plan. Interior Minister Clifford Sifton initiated an ambitious advertising campaign that blatantly challenged the United States by calling Canada "The Last Best West." Hundreds of Ottawa-appointed immigration agents were hired and dispatched to European and Canadian cities. People were offered cheap or free passage over the ocean and then across Canada to accept the irresistibly intoxicating gift of 160 acres of free land. It worked. They came. Between 1901 and 1911, about two million people came. Many brought small packets of earth from home to mix into their new Canadian homesteads.

Canada's growth and security were helped by another federal government initiative. In 1886, Macdonald had appointed Dr. William Saunders as the first director of the federal government's Central Experimental Farms Service. Its purpose was to research and resolve the agricultural challenges of Canada's cold climate. Saunders travelled the country to work with various strains of wheat while hybridizing others.

The Laurier government continued to support his efforts until finally, after years of research, Saunders developed Marquis wheat. It was shorter and so better able to withstand damaging Prairie winds. Because it matured seven to ten days earlier than other strains, it had a better chance of avoiding late and early frosts. It also yielded more per acre. The federal government program that resulted in the invention of Marquis wheat allowed Prairie economies to develop and led to Canada becoming among the world's greatest suppliers of wheat. It gave thousands of new Canadians, attracted by Laurier's sales campaign, a better chance at success. It made them less likely to slip south of the border and provided those considering the Atlantic trek to "the last, best west" an even stronger incentive to embark.

With all the federal government's ambitious actions, the West grew. Businesses, cities, and towns spotted along the CPR tracks through the wide Prairie and hugging the Great Lakes and St. Lawrence shores also grew. In fact, about half of the new Canadians settled in growing urban centres that became the backbone of nascent resource development industries, especially mining, steel, and lumber. The federal government's efforts that spurred the growth in population, wealth, infrastructure, and the economy resulted in the creation of Alberta and Saskatchewan in 1905. The new provinces, along with development in British Columbia and Manitoba, boosted Canada's sovereignty and drove nails into Manifest Destiny's coffin.

While building the country, the federal government also needed to continue its efforts to save Canada from provincial pressures still intent on tearing the nation's fabric. Manitoba had become a province in 1870 through the inspired but unstable leadership of Louis Riel. His legacy of protecting minority religious rights was threatened when, in 1890, Manitoba abolished Catholic education. Because the law went to Confederation's heart, the federal government opposed it and off it went to the JCPC. The Lords let the law stand but said the federal government could disallow it. Manitoba refused to budge. Quebec recognized this as an attack on religious and language rights and demanded action. Ontario split along religious lines, with each side screaming betrayal. Conservative federal governments held their breath and did nothing in the face of a shattering national unity. Then Laurier was elected.

Laurier negotiated a compromise with the Manitoba premier that allowed fired Catholic teachers to be reinstated and Catholic kids to be taught where numbers warranted. Manitoba saved face, Quebec felt vindicated, and Ontario's wounds were salved. Due to the cleverness of the national leader, the genie of Canadian divisions and disunity was stuffed back in the bottle. It would not stay put for long. British demands pulled it out again.

Since the end of the American Civil War threats, Canada had allowed its military preparedness to wane to laughable lows. In 1904, Laurier yielded to political pressure to protect fishing vessels and had his government buy and outfit eight small ships. Months later, the British government announced that due to its expensive responses to Germany's growing naval threat, its ships and men were being recalled from Halifax on one coast and Esquimalt on the other. Five years later, with the naval race gaining momentum, Britain asked its colonies for ships.

Many English-speaking imperialists, mostly in the Maritimes, British Columbia, and Ontario, demanded obedience. Quebec's French-speaking nationalists wanted Britain rebuffed. In 1910, Laurier presented his compromise: the Naval Service Bill. Ships would be built and a small Canadian navy established with the promise that it would support Britain if war ever came. Laurier had again walked the Sunny Way of compromise and kept the country together even as war seemed imminent. No one guessed it would come so soon.

The Great War, so called for its scope and not magnificence, shone a blinding light on the cleavages dividing the country and on the ever-present question of power. After decades of the British Lords and the provinces carving away slices of Ottawa's power, the sudden crisis meant they needed it to be suddenly powerful again. The job would be immense. The federal government rallied itself and the country.

Not all Canadians wanted war. Western farmers worried about losing their sons, who were loved, of course, but also essential to the family business. Many French-speaking Quebecers opposed the imperial war. But the country had no choice. We were not threatened by Europe's arms race, nationalist nattering, and imperialist land grabs, but when, in August 1914, Britain declared war, we were automatically at war.

Laurier had lost office in 1911 with a failed attempt to sell his plan for free trade with the Americans. Robert Borden had become prime minister and just three years later was Canada's wartime leader. Borden declared Canada "Ready, Aye, Ready," but the country wasn't even close. Its new and tiny "Tin Pot" navy was hardly a potent force, and its army consisted of only about 3,000 men and 43,000 ill-trained militia. The bureaucratic, legal, and financial challenges of putting an army in the field and a navy at sea were overwhelming.

Borden stabilized banks and financial institutions by declaring that national currency, and not the banknotes that were common at the time, would pay for all war costs. The federal government then set about building its military. Initially, a good deal was botched. More than 30,000 volunteers overwhelmed the government's ability to feed, clothe, train, and ship them. Too many of the political appointees put in place to manage the war found ambitions outpacing skills, which led to bad decisions, faulty equipment and weapons, missed deadlines, and cost overruns. Everyone learned as they went, incompetents were fired, and systems were created. Starting from nothing at all, the federal government coordinated private enterprise activity and created a munitions industry. By February 1915, the Canadian contingent of 18,000 volunteer civilian-soldiers was deployed on the Western Front. Thousands more were being trained to follow. A country of only eight million mostly agrarian people had stunningly rallied itself to feed the biggest and most mechanized monster of a war the world had ever seen. But it was not enough.

Prime Minister Borden visited London in 1915 and was shocked to learn details regarding the stalemated, bloody, muddy Western Front. Neither side could win, but neither could lose, so they kept fighting. Young men continued to be pushed into no man's land with a belly full of rum and no hope. Others flew rickety planes that fell as fireballs from the sky. Thousands returned home with ghastly wounds and missing limbs, and more with emotional scars no one could see but from which there was no reprieve. The war killed men and families long after the massacre stopped.

In his 1916 New Year's message to Canadians, Borden pledged a half million more soldiers. But the volunteer well was running dry. The problem was especially acute in Quebec. The rate of volunteers among young Quebecers was similar to all other provinces at the outset of the war, but in 1913 the Ontario government passed Regulation 17, and its implementation began at the same time as the first recruitment drives. The regulation restricted French-language instruction in Ontario. Quebec MPs brought the regulation to a fiery House of Commons debate, but Ontario refused to back down. In February 1916, 5,000 angry French-speaking protesters were on Parliament Hill. Henri Bourassa, Quebec nationalist and founder-editor of the opinion-shaping *Le Devoir*, spoke for many when he said that Quebecers were fighting a war against Germans and "Prussians in Ontario."[1] The already palpable tension was made worse when Bourassa's remarks led many English Canadians and English-language newspapers to brand him and Quebecers as unpatriotic traitors. The Ontario government's action and its predictable backlash led to a decline in Quebec recruitment just as Borden needed more soldiers.

After attending the Imperial War Conference in London and then visiting the dismal, tragic trenches again in the spring of 1917, Borden announced the necessity to fill the dwindling ranks through conscription. Every Quebec member of Parliament opposed the Military Service Act that made conscription the law of the land. Every provincial legislature except Quebec's and nearly every English-speaking MP supported it. While Liberal opposition leader Laurier would not join, Borden created a coalition government to pass the conscription bill. There were cheers in many cities. There were grumbles and curses in many farm kitchens. There were riots in Quebec City. Soldiers from Ontario were taunted in French and then pelted with snowballs. They overreacted and fired into a crowd. Many were wounded and four were killed.

By the war's end in November 1918, conscription had forced 124,588 into uniform, and of their ranks 24,132 suffered the front. Conscription has been described as a waste in light of the relatively few soldiers it added to Canada's military might so late in the war. However, no one at the time knew when or how the war would end. If the Americans had not entered, Austria-Hungary had not revolted, or Germany had reacted differently to Russia's withdrawal, the war could have dragged on and Canadian conscription might have been accepted as an evil necessary to fight an ongoing evil.

Politically, conscription was a catastrophe. The federal government that was primarily responsible for keeping the country together had deepened fissures that would take generations to heal. Yet, enough people supported conscription that Borden was re-elected after the war. Regardless of one's interpretation of conscription as a military and political matter, its demonstration of Ottawa's ability to meet an emergency, even clumsily, cannot be denied.

In fact, the concept of emergency was exactly what afforded the government the constitutional power to enact conscription and take other actions deemed necessary to fight the war. In 1914, Borden passed the War Measures Act. It allowed the federal cabinet to temporarily suspend civil rights. Some of the actions taken under the act's authority were misguided. Those deemed enemy aliens, for instance, were arrested and interned. The federal government was able to all but ignore Parliament while also intervening as never before in the economy. It passed many far-reaching orders-in-council that, officially, are directives from the governor general but, in fact, come from the prime minister and cabinet. They are decrees with the force of law that do not require the consent of Parliament. Borden's cabinet issued orders-in-council that, for example, forced many private companies to stop manufacturing some products, such as cars and farm implements, and instead retool to build armaments.

Many orders-in-council were challenged by the provinces with the old tactic of skipping through or around the Supreme Court to the Judicial Committee of the Privy Council. However, its decades-long shifting of power to the provinces was suspended to let Ottawa lead the war effort. In each case brought before it during the war, the JCPC ruled that the federal government's emergency measures were temporary and necessary and so were allowed to stand.

While tending to these important matters, Canada contributed enormously to Britain's war effort. In 1915, Prime Minister Borden recommended that Britain's Canadian-based Imperial Munitions Board (IMB) be run by Canadian businessman Joseph Flavelle. Soon there were 30,000 men and women administering an efficient operation that included Crown corporations and private companies. Six hundred factories with 250,000 employees produced $2 million worth of war materiel a day. By the end of 1917, the IMB was producing a third of all British shells. It built 88 ships and 2,900 planes. Beyond that, Canadian food made up portions of at least half of all British civilian meals.

The effort was impressive, but expensive. Ottawa's pre-war budget was only $185 million. By the middle of the war, it was $740 million. Borden's government did what all governments do when similarly strapped — it borrowed the money. The borrowing began with Britain, with the funds boomeranged back as soldiers, food, and weaponry. Federal debt rose quickly and steadily from $463 million before the war to $2.5 billion in 1918. Borden was shocked when informed that Britain's ballooning debt was such that it could no longer afford to help Canada help the war effort.

Borden had few good options and the best of the worst was to turn to the United States. The loans came. He also turned to Canadians, and people jumped at the chance to contribute. The greatest success previously had been the raising of $5 million, but in 1917 alone, Canadians purchased $300 million worth of Victory Bonds. The 5 percent interest attracted some, but most folks said they simply wanted to help. By the war's end, $2 billion had been raised.

The American and bond loans were good, but not enough. Borden approved new business taxes and then, in 1917, came Canada's first income tax on individuals. He promised that it was just a temporary measure to pay for the war. The JCPC was asked to rule on the tax's constitutionality, and it again cited wartime emergency as a reason to allow this new exertion of federal power. Income tax rates were low and exemptions generous, but an important step had been taken. At the war's end, income tax accounted for only 3.4 percent of federal revenue, but the tax became permanent, created a new revenue stream, and increased capacity for future activity.

VIMY'S ECHO

It was Easter Monday 1917. For the Canadians dug into the stinking squalor of muddy trenches or crouching in long and elaborate tunnels, there would be no time for observance.

Rum was swallowed, hands were shaken, prayers were offered, and dark jokes shared. The big, deafening guns began their roar on time and ripped the air. At 5:30 a.m., 15,000 men rose as one and trudged slowly forward, ignoring the cold, sleet, mud, and fear.

Vimy Ridge is four miles long and stands 196 feet above an otherwise flat and open plain near Arras, France. German forces had held the important high ground since the beginning of the war, British and French troops had already died by the score trying to push them off. Now the Canadians would try. They had planned and trained for weeks, with every man learning his job. It would be the first time that all four Canadian divisions would fight together as one.

By early afternoon, the slowly rising ridge was littered with badly mangled bodies and thousands of wounded young men crying out, as suffering soldiers always do, for their mothers. Seven thousand Canadian wounded were carried from the charred field that day and 3,598 died. But Canadians were atop the ridge.

All Canadians owe it to themselves to visit Vimy and stand by the preserved trenches, walk the tunnels, observe the graves, and marvel at the towering, gleaming white monument, feeling the compelling contradiction of revulsion and pride. Or they can simply stay home, and to paraphrase what was once said of the architect who created London's St. Paul's Cathedral, seek the monument to those men who fought on that cold Easter Monday so long ago by just looking around.

The battle of Vimy Ridge entered Canadian mythology. Sure, the overall commander was British, British artillerymen and engineers were involved, and the Germans quickly adjusted and fought for another 19 months, but to Canadians back home at the time, hardened by years of sad and bad news, Vimy offered not just the sunshine of success, but the warmth of it having been a Canadian success. Brigadier-General Alexander Ross observed, "In those few minutes I witnessed the birth of a nation."

Myths matter. When considered collectively with the sacrifice of so many in the war that many still hoped might end all wars, the Vimy myth swells with significance. The war saw nearly 620,000 Canadians don uniforms, with an astounding 37 percent wounded or killed. More than 61,000 died. Over 172,000 suffered life-changing wounds, with 3,400 losing a limb and more than 9,000 suffering from what was then called shell shock. Most Canadians still considered themselves loyal British subjects, and legally they were. But in their hearts, where nationhood truly matters, more and more found that Vimy and the war had turned them into Canadians.

Through his handling of postwar negotiations, it fell to Prime Minister Robert Borden to use the power of the federal government to provide voice to the growing national pride and honour the sacrifice of so many brave Canadians. For six months, beginning in the summer of 1919, the victors gathered at Versailles. To clear the smoke of war, the opulent palace's Hall of Mirrors was unintentionally appropriate to host a conference of the victors but where the Big Three — United States, Britain, and France — called the shots. Like all other countries, Canada played a small role. When it came time to sign the treaty, Borden insisted but lost the right to sign as an independent state. Britain signed for all its dominions but in a concession to their contributions and evolving status, at least each was allowed to sign in an indented list below.

Borden was more successful in enhancing Canada's sovereignty with the League of Nations. A Treaty of Versailles covenant created the league that, it was hoped, would protect borders and encourage countries to resolve differences through discussion rather than war. Britain said it would represent all imperial interests at league meetings. Borden reminded British leaders that at an Imperial War Conference in 1917 he had demanded and won recognition of the dominions as separate entities with separate interests. With support from Australia and South Africa, Borden pushed the point and Canada became one of 63 independent League of Nations member states.

The United States objected to Canada's role, but was reminded that while it joined the war in its final months, Canada had fought from the beginning and lost more lives. Canadian financier Sir Herbert Ames served as the league's financial director from 1919 to 1926, and Canada was elected to serve as a non-permanent member of the league's decision-making council from 1927 to 1930. The league was doomed to failure, but Canada's participation was nonetheless another important recognition of its wartime sacrifices, of its growing autonomy, and of the sun slowly setting on Britain's power in the world and over its former North American colonies.

The same factors were in play when, in 1922, Britain asked for help from the dominions after Turkish troops threatened a British occupying force at Chanak, a strategically important seaport on the Dardanelles Strait. Prime Minister William Lyon Mackenzie King, newly installed in office, responded that Canada's Parliament would decide upon Canadian involvement. Parliament debated and said Canada would not send help to Chanak.

Canada's temerity in not immediately jumping to the call of empire was considered a disloyal travesty by British Prime Minister David Lloyd George and Colonial Secretary Winston Churchill. Churchill's anachronistic title alone should have tipped Westminster about Ottawa's problem, but old perceptions, like habits, die slow and hard. It was not the first time Canada had balked at British demands. In 1899, Laurier said no to troops but then agreed to support volunteers who wished to fight British battles against South African Boers. A few years later, he offered neither money nor ships but the country's small navy to assist Britain. But Chanak was different. This time, and for the first time, Canada flatly said no.

Only a year after King had stood up to the British in the Chanak Affair, a dispute over fishing rights on the North Pacific coast brought Americans and Canadians to the bargaining table. Britain insisted on participating and co-signing any agreement. King again said no. In March 1923, Canada and the United States signed the Halibut Treaty. It established Canada's right to independently negotiate and conclude commercial treaties. The treaty was yet another demonstration that, in matters of the heart, head, and wallet, the federal government's bold leadership had moved Canada farther from Britain. The country was striding ever more confidently toward full sovereignty. Indeed, the prime minister dined with the governor general on the evening the Halibut Treaty was signed. They agreed that it had, in King's words, removed from Canada the "badge of colonialism." And King was not done distancing Canada from the King.

The prime minister appointed the highly respected O.D. Skelton as undersecretary of state for external affairs. He asked Skelton to expand the tiny department. Skelton was a brilliant administrator and set up the people and structure that allowed Canada to take further steps from Britain's shadow. The first diplomatic mission was established in Washington, D.C., and was led by Vincent Massey, a future governor general.

Then, in 1926, King attended a momentous imperial conference. It was chaired by Lord Balfour, former British prime minister and respected foreign secretary. The wise 78-year-old Brit immediately acknowledged the elephant in the room by stating that the First World War had radically shifted the world's power structure and the relationships between Britain and its former colonies. He said the war left the manner in which members of the empire were to interact "unexplained and undefined." Everyone in British political circles knew that Lord Balfour's career had been given enormous help by his influential uncle, Lord Robert Cecil. It is the source of the aphorism dedicated to unearned nepotism: "Bob's your uncle."

King was an active participant in the 15 meetings that discussed options regarding a new relationship. The creation of a written imperial constitution was considered but declined in favour of a more British principled understanding. It was established that each member, including, most importantly, Britain itself, should be equal in status. The Balfour Report said the British Parliament should surrender its right to pass legislation binding on the dominions unless directly asked to do so. If the report's recommendations were accepted, Canada would join the other dominions in taking a giant leap toward full sovereignty.

The Balfour Report was being debated when Prime Minister R.B. Bennett took office in October 1930. It was quickly accepted in Britain and in the other dominions, but in Canada, the provinces didn't like it. Leading the charge against the nation-building initiative was Ontario Premier Howard Ferguson. He sent a long letter to Bennett arguing that the Balfour Report was less about earning Canadian independence from Britain and more about Ottawa grabbing power to dominate the provinces. Ferguson's real complaint, and that of other premiers who supported him, especially those from Saskatchewan, British Columbia, and Quebec, was that the new status of the dominions would necessitate the end of Britain's 1865 Colonial Laws Validity Act. The act stated that neither the federal nor any of the provincial governments could pass a law that was deemed contradictory to British law, or as it stated, was "repugnant" to British interests. The premiers understood and liked that the Validity Act was a check on the federal government's power just as the Constitution's power of disallowance was a check on theirs. The provinces' perhaps unintentional point was that they accepted Canada having more independence when it didn't threaten their powers, such as participating in the war or the League of Nations, but they drew the line if Canada's becoming more legally and constitutionally independent could potentially threaten their powers.

Premier Ferguson called Canada's Constitution a provincial treaty. The federal government, he wrote, had no right to change Canada's legal relationship with Britain because it would effectively be rewriting that treaty. Bennett was left with the option of taking the bold steps toward Canadian independence or being the only dominion to refuse to do so due to provincial parochialism. He opted to compromise. After long discussions in cabinet, Canada joined all the other dominions and moved toward the implementation of the Balfour Report recommendations. However, Bennett allowed progress to be made and the provinces to save face by watering the wine of sovereignty that would be enjoyed by all the other former colonies. The Colonial Laws Validity Act would remain for Canada alone and Britain would maintain control of Canada's guiding, defining document, its Constitution. If amendments were needed in the future, Canada would ask the British Parliament to make them, since the Constitution would remain a British law. The Judicial Committee of the Privy Council would retain its power to overturn Canadian Supreme Court decisions.

At an imperial conference held in December 1931, Canada signed the Statute of Westminster, which put the Balfour Report into practice. It effectively killed the old British Empire and midwifed the Commonwealth of Nations. Perhaps even more than Confederation, and despite provincial objections that led to lingering colonial remnants, the Statute of Westminster was Canada's declaration of independence.

Besides tripping up the federal government's attempt at fuller sovereignty, the provinces also renewed their unspoken alliance with the JCPC to steal what they could from Ottawa's power. Because the emergency of war was over, the JCPC Lords returned to reimagining Sir John's intentions by resuming its shifting of power from the centre. An important indication of the old trend becoming new again was the 1919 Board of Commerce case.

After the war's conclusion, the federal government passed the Board of Commerce Act and the Combines and Fair Prices Act. The laws sought to control unfair profits and regulate mergers and monopolies. The provinces saw the laws as stepping on their ground and fought them with a case that eventually landed with the Lords. The JCPC had allowed similar action to stand during the war but repeated its earlier ruling that only in circumstances of national emergency such as famine or war could the federal government use Section 91's Peace, Order, and Good Government clause to impinge on provincial trade and commerce power. While the profiteering businessmen were certainly unethical and immoral, their actions did not rise to the level of a national emergency in peacetime, and therefore the federal laws were deemed unconstitutional.

Another sign of the JCPC retaking its position in the provincial corner and pushing a decentralized Canada was seen when the federal government intervened to settle a strike involving the Toronto Electric Commission. The Ontario government welcomed the strike's settlement. However, it complained that the federal action violated its power to control property and civil rights. The 1925 *Toronto Electric Commissioners v. Snider* case landed with the JCPC, which sided with Ontario, again on the basis of the situation not constituting a national emergency.

The two cases were significant because they signalled that the return of peace had brought back the narrow interpretation of the Peace, Order, and Good Government clause. The JCPC had already determined that the clause was separate from Section 91's list of Ottawa's powers that followed and constituted a strict definition of its precise limits. The JCPC was now suggesting that very little would be allowed to justify invoking the Peace, Order, and Good Government clause in the future, and so federal power would be corralled.

As always, however, while working to limit Ottawa's power, the provinces remained willing to call upon it. Such a call came from Manitoba in May 1919. Winnipeg was Canada's third-largest city and had sent the greatest percentage of any city's population to the war. Like nearly everywhere, the clumsy beating of swords into ploughshares had brought Winnipeg's citizens unemployment and runaway inflation. The city's Trades and Labour Council opted to protest those they decided to blame for hard times by calling a general strike. The response was astounding. Within hours, 30,000 people were off the job, including factory workers, secretaries, phone operators, and more disturbingly, garbage collectors, police officers, firefighters, and waterworks engineers. Municipal politicians joined bankers and industrialists in condemning the strikers as Communists. Racist elements blamed immigrants. Veterans fought, sometimes with violence, for the rights and recognition their service had earned. With so many sides to the complex mess, Winnipeg's mayor and council were quickly overwhelmed. Manitoba Premier T.C. Norris fumed but did nothing, except ask for Ottawa's help.

Federal Minister of Labour Gideon Robertson and Arthur Meighen, acting minister of justice and future prime minister, were dispatched to address the crisis. They did their best, but none of the various factions would give ground. With more violence brewing and openly advocated, Robertson and Meighen expressed support for the politicians and business leaders. The Canadian Criminal Code was amended to allow for the arrest of strike leaders on the charge of sedition. A large and specially empowered police force was created, and the T. Eaton Company supplied it with horses and baseball bats. A confrontation was coming. On June 17, a crowd gathered downtown to protest the arrests and plan further action. Royal North-West Mounted Police officers incited a riot. Bones and teeth were broken, and blood was spilled. One striker was killed.

The strikes ended shortly afterward. The riot was an avoidable tragedy. Canadians were appalled. The strike and riot demonstrated that when called upon, the federal government had the legitimacy, authority, and power to intervene in situations where municipal and provincial governments could not, or, as in this case, would not. With this said, the people of Winnipeg in 1919 were like those in Regina in 1935, many in Montreal in 1970, and generations of Aboriginal people who suffered at residential schools; all would attest that Ottawa was capable of acting decisively but in doing so it sometimes misunderstood and mishandled a situation and so misused its power.

Alcohol seldom clarifies much, but during and after the war, it certainly made clear the limits of provincial power on a national scale. There had been groups urging a ban on alcohol even before Confederation, but beyond some largely ineffective legislation, such as the 1864 Dunkin Act, not much had been done. The Women's Christian Temperance Union (WCTU) was created in Owen Sound, Ontario, in 1874. By the 1890s, it had become a powerful force in a number of cities. The movement's determination and the support of premiers led the federal government to create the Royal Commission on the Liquor Traffic. In 1895, it recommended against a national alcohol ban. The commission found that the constitutional basis for Ottawa's capping of the spigots was as "questionable" as its ability to ever enforce prohibition laws was "illusory." The federal government considered the warnings and did perhaps the wisest thing by doing nothing.

Premiers, however, ignored the Royal Commission and Ottawa. Manitoba, Prince Edward Island, Nova Scotia, and then Ontario ran provincial plebiscites. Unlike a referendum, which legally binds the government to act on whatever is decided by the electorate, a plebiscite is akin to a poll that merely solicits citizens' opinions through a yes or no vote. In all four cases, majorities voted to ban booze. In fact, in none of the provinces was the voting even close. In Manitoba, for example, the first province to go to its people, 19,637 voted for prohibition with only 7,115 against.

Prohibition supporters were pleased with Wilfrid Laurier's election in 1896 because the Liberal Party's platform had promised a national plebiscite. Laurier delayed as long as he could, but pressure from the WCTU and some premiers was relentless. The plebiscite was called. Some cities and towns heard little about it while campaigns elsewhere were well financed and scrupulously organized. On September 29, 1898, for the first time, Canadians went to polling stations to express their opinions on a single issue.

The people's voice was heard, but it was tough to understand what was said. Only 44 percent bothered to vote, and of those, 51 percent voted in favour of prohibition and 49 percent against. While 87 percent of Nova Scotians voted yes, only 19 percent of Quebecers wanted to cork their bottles. Laurier decided that the low turnout, narrow margin, and vastly different responses in different provinces meant that no consensus existed, so he refused to act.

The fight smouldered until the European war. Those who had long advocated prohibition began to use the war to sell their beliefs as patriotism. How, it was asked, could grain that could be food be wasted on alcohol, and how could people be wasting time and lives drinking when so much sacrifice was being offered in Flanders?

Prince Edward Island had enacted a prohibition law in 1901. Beginning in 1915, though, one province after another passed similar laws. By 1917, every province and Yukon Territory had passed laws according to their constitutional powers to regulate the consumption and sale of the stuff. Ottawa still controlled alcohol's manufacture and trade. In March 1918, with the war still raging, Robert Borden's government supported all the provincial legislation with the National Prohibition Act, passed under the auspices of the War Measures Act.

The end of the war ended the federal government's participation. Quebec withdrew its law and threw open its bars. The other provinces, however, stuck to their guns after the Europeans packed up theirs. Ottawa's withdrawal from the prohibition experiment left a hodgepodge of provincial laws and regulations. The many exceptions to the rules made many of the rules silly. For example, provinces allowed physicians to prescribe alcohol-laced medicine and pretended not to notice the long lines snaking outside doctor's offices on Fridays and before holidays.

Illegally running liquor to the United States, which had nationally mandated prohibition laws, became big business. A Lunenburg fisherman could make more money from a couple of rum runs to Boston than a full season of tending nets or traps. Even the era's most notorious criminal, Chicago's Al Capone, worked provincial laws. He was rumoured to be operating in many Canadian cities and even in tunnels beneath Moose Jaw, Saskatchewan. When asked about his Canadian connections, Capone laconically replied, "I don't even know what street Canada is on."

Premiers soon realized the wisdom of the federal

government's Royal Commission warning that prohibition's enforcement would be impossible, Laurier's opinion that it was inadvisable, and Borden's decision to end Ottawa's involvement with the war's conclusion. Beginning with British Columbia in 1921, provincial prohibition laws were revoked. By 1929, only Prince Edward Island, surrounded by water, stayed dry. It would do so until 1948. A smattering of cities and towns enacted bylaws banning booze, some of which lingered for decades.

Prohibition offers many lessons. It is tough to legislate morality. Supply will always meet demand. Also learned was that no matter how well intentioned or carefully implemented the plan, the provinces can't create a national program. The failures and unintended consequences of the provinces' prohibition gambit were unfortunate. Even as provinces walked back their laws and folks were again able to enjoy a legal drink, Canadians had no way of knowing that the provincial and federal government's ability to respond to an emergency was about to be tested in a new and devastating crisis like it had not been tested before. They would need that drink.

3

THE CRASH

The 1920s were unfair. The roaring roller coaster that brought the best of times to many with new music, fashion, and prosperity visited the worst of times upon others with racism, crime, violence, and poverty. The wild ride went off the rails in late 1929, hurtling nearly all riders into the abyss. The 1930s were even more unfair and to even more people.

Consider the startling statistics while remembering the lives lost in the numbers. In 1928, Saskatchewan produced 321 million bushels of wheat. Two years later, due to plummeting prices, repossessed farms, a drought, and a biblical plague of locusts, production fell to 132 million bushels. The annual net income for a Saskatchewan farm sank from $1,614 to an astonishing $66. A year of back-breaking work on the average New Brunswick farm earned only $20. From 1928 to 1933, the value of all fish caught in the three Maritime provinces was halved from $20 million to $10 million. Many fishermen cut costs by returning to sails while others cut losses and left.

City folks were similarly hit. The national average annual wage fell by 48 percent. The Ford Motor Company reported sales of $46 million in 1930 but two years later only $17 million. It reduced costs by dismissing workers and cutting production, but many other companies, both big and small, locked their gates, leaving creditors with little and workers with less. The national unemployment rate rocketed from 3 percent in 1929 to 30 percent in 1931, but everyone knew it was probably higher. Ontario's unemployment rate hit 45 percent. Men risked arrest and their lives to hop atop trains to head west seeking work. They passed equally desperate men heading east. There was no work. There was no hope. The only certainty was that the old adage was wrong: misery does not really like company, after all.

The Depression gobsmacked all three levels of government. Plunging tax revenues led municipal governments to cut wages and hours, lay off workers, and reduce or end services. In British Columbia alone, Burnaby, Merritt, Prince Rupert, and North Vancouver declared bankruptcy. Meanwhile, growing numbers of homeless, destitute people, along with the hungry migrant unemployed, swamped locally funded and organized relief efforts.

The BNA Act made the provinces responsible for welfare, and they attempted to meet their responsibilities, but fiscal realities rendered it first difficult and then impossible as revenues plummeted. In two years, the Saskatchewan government, for instance, saw its income fall by 90 percent. All provinces eventually joined British Columbia and Prince Edward Island in levying corporate taxes. They hiked gasoline taxes; raised succession duties; and Ontario, Quebec, Saskatchewan, and Alberta introduced an income tax. None of it was enough. **With provincial revenues continuing to shrink as dramatically** as spending ballooned, and with no end to tough times in sight, fewer wanted their bonds and so even borrowing to meet obligations ceased to be an option.

The Depression proved once again that no matter how well led or nobly intentioned, provinces simply cannot address catastrophic emergencies. Premiers did what they always do in times of crisis. They did their best and then called Ottawa for help. In one of the few instances of his political instincts failing him, Prime Minister King decided that the best thing he could do was nothing at all. The Liberals took a conservative approach. King insisted that unemployment would decline when companies eventually responded to shortages with increased production. Government's job, he insisted, was to stay out of the way while markets righted themselves.

Even if King had been correct, he daggered his argument by appearing to lack compassion for those left waiting for the righting. He was asked in the House of Commons to respond to provincial demands for Ottawa's help and replied:

> So far as money from this Federal Treasury to the provincial governments is concerned, in relation to the question of unemployment as it exists today, I might be prepared to go a certain length possibly in meeting one or two of the western provinces that have Progressive premiers at the head of their governments … but I would not give a single cent to any Tory government.[1]

There were gasps among the honourable members. He had time to think and recover but then, in a direct response to a B.C. MP yelling "Shame," he doubled down by shouting,

"May I repeat what I have said … while these governments are situated as they are today with politics diametrically opposed to this government, I would not give them a five-cent piece."[2] Canadians tolerated power squabbles between Ottawa and the provinces, but were repulsed when fights became blindly partisan and so more about the squabblers than the people.

Within months, King called an election and the Liberals were soundly defeated. In October 1930, R.B. Bennett, the multi-millionaire Calgary lawyer who had captured the Conservative Party leadership in 1927, earned a massive majority with 56 percent of the popular vote. Bennett was a spectacular campaigner and remarkable public speaker. He won the day with promises to "attack" unemployment and "blast" his way into world markets. Canadians were hurting and had turned to a national leader promising national action.

A misguided notion is that government should be run like a business. A majority of businesses are out of business in their first five years and even big businesses go bust — remember Eaton's? Businesses exist to attract consumers and make money. A state, and governments within them, must endure. They exist not to enrich themselves, but to serve citizens and protect rights. For citizens, more than employees, investors, or consumers, government is the voice and enabler of community.

Community is a feeling. It grows from shared values, interests, experiences, and goals. We are social animals and so we naturally seek community. It is the yearning that leads some to churches and others to street gangs. It is the warmth and smiles of a book club or a slow-pitch ball team.

A national community is dynamic. Most of us are born, live, and die in one country. We find community in implicitly accepting the power of the state, debating current government actions and politicians, and in the embrace of values that link "we the people" — the nation. It is community that brings us to our feet for the anthem and after a trip abroad makes the flag look so good.

The question of community is one of circles. Does the circle of people for whom we feel affinity and responsibility end at ourselves, our family, city, province, region, or country? If the circle ends only with those with whom we share a last name, then there is no need or justification for collective action to help others. On the other hand, if the circle is more broadly drawn, then churches, charities, and other organs and avenues of the local civil society become involved to meet greater needs. If the circle becomes even larger, then the provincial and ultimately the national government must assume roles. Where we circumscribe our circle thereby influences our feelings about government and the use of our tax dollars to support its power and role in our society. These questions always matter, but they become especially acute in times of emergency such as an economic collapse. Answering the questions of circles and community lead to more questions about the degree to which Sir John's power structure was up to the job of addressing such a dire emergency.

The Depression's ravages were so devastating and widespread, its causes so complex, and its solutions so elusive, that families, then churches and charities, and then local and provincial governments were bamboozled. The circles simply had to radiate outward. The federal government had to step up and use its power to meet the crisis. When far too many Canadian children whisper of hunger when being tucked into bed, ideological debates about the role of government and of the constitutional niceties of federalism seem unseemly. It was what made King's five-cent speech such a calamitous blunder. The circles were redrawn.

While Sir John and the founders had made provinces responsible for welfare, the word's definition was vague, with no one guessing how its meaning would evolve. Responsibility for well-being had turned into calls for programs addressing income redistribution with guarantees of a certain level of material comfort for all. The British government had passed the Unemployment Insurance Act in 1911. The action spurred Canadian talk of similar legislation, but the war interrupted the conversation. It resumed afterward with Borden's government seeking to help integrate soldiers back into society with the Employment Officers Co-ordination Act. It also passed the Department of Employment Services, which gathered and shared employment data and sent money to provincial governments to help with job-creation projects.

Borden also created a Royal Commission to investigate worker-industry relations. Among its June 1919 recommendations was this: "We recommend to your Government the question of making some provision by a system of State Social Insurance for those who through no fault of their own are unable to work, whether the inability arises from lack of opportunity, sickness, invalidity or old age. Such insurance would remove the spectre of fear which now haunts the wage earner and make him a more contented and a better citizen."

The notion seems reasonable now, but at the time it was revolutionary. It was asking the federal government to take even more responsibility for the welfare of Canadians and to nudge further into the provincial sphere. It took six years, but the political courage was finally mustered to nudge away.

In 1927, federal legislation introduced a national old-age pension program. It was tentative. Pensions were capped at $20 per month and made available only to British subjects over the age of 70 who had lived in Canada for 20 years and made less than $365 a year. Status Indians could not apply. To alleviate jurisdictional squabbles, the law afforded each province the option of becoming a part of the national program. Slowly, different provinces accepted Ottawa's money, and a patchwork quilt of a program to help poor seniors was implemented.

The King government worked to build on the limited success of the old-age pension program when, in 1929, premiers were consulted about the possibility of creating a similar program of unemployment insurance. They pushed back. When stock markets crashed a few months later, the pushing stopped.

After Bennett's election, action came quickly. A special session of Parliament passed the Unemployment Relief Act. It shovelled money into projects that promised to put shovels in the ground. Roads, bridges, railways, canals, and more would be built. Furthermore, the act reimbursed municipal and provincial governments that were going broke trying to finance their direct-relief programs. The provinces happily accepted the money. British Columbia led other provinces in initiating make-work infrastructure projects of their own that added to the effectiveness of the federal government's actions.

Bennett's initiatives to help Canadians and their provincial and municipal governments were budgeted for $20 million. That seems paltry by 21st-century standards, but it was a substantial sum when one notes that Ottawa's budget at the time was only $500 million. A year later, the Unemployment and Farm Relief Act extended the first act's term and reach. Bennett's actions were a further declaration that the federal government saw the welfare of individual Canadians as not a family, local, or provincial concern, but a national responsibility.

Meanwhile, with immediate relief being doled out, the federal government moved to address not just the Depression's effects, but also its causes. Like President Roosevelt would in the United States, Bennett knew that changes were needed to save people from the effects of excruciating economic troughs and capitalism from itself. He began with trade.

The Great Depression was caused by a number of factors and among them was the suffocation of global trade through actions such as America's highly restrictive Smoot-Hawley Tariff. In an attempt to protect domestic industries, the U.S. government's new tariffs spurred similar protectionist actions around the world until by 1933 world trade was two-thirds lower than it had been in 1929. Canada's foreign trade, then as now the foundation of the country's wealth, dropped by 65 percent.

Bennett did what he could to break trade barriers. At a London conference that convened three months after he took office, the prime minister blustered, bullied, and convinced Commonwealth leaders to come to Ottawa. They met in the House of Commons and negotiations were long and tough. While the results were disappointing, a number of tariffs were dropped, which allowed more Canadian wheat and grain to be sold to Commonwealth countries. Deals discussed in Ottawa were later inked. Within two years, Canadian trade to Britain had risen 10 percent and to other Commonwealth countries by 12 percent.

Roosevelt became president in 1933 and immediately embarked on a program of legislation dubbed the New Deal. It essentially mirrored Bennett's plan, first offering relief to address immediate needs and then making structural changes to mitigate future downturns. In 1935, the last year of his administration, Bennett oversaw trade negotiations with the United States. A new trade deal was ready except for minor details when Bennett was swept from power. The new prime minister, actually the old prime minister returned to office, Mackenzie King, had little left to do but sign his name. Together with the Commonwealth trade deals and others with other countries, the American agreement expanded markets, created new ones, and brought jobs and dignity to many suffering Canadians.

Another element of Ottawa seeking to address the Depression's causes was Bennett's wrestling control of Canada's monetary policy from the chartered banks. While fiscal policy involves money coming into and going out of government, monetary policy involves the overall number of dollars in play. When the Depression's shadow darkened Canada, Canadian wallets carried Canadian money but also legal currency from the Bank of Montreal, the Bank of Commerce, and the others. In the 1920s, chartered bank bills made up nearly half of the currency in circulation. Banks also manipulated how many dollars were in circulation by raising interest rates to tighten credit or lowering them to make credit easier. The banks regulated the relative worth of Canada's currency in global money markets. The federal government ensured through law and regulation that banks matched the amount of dollars they printed with gold they owned and locked in reserve.

Financing the First World War had put an enormous strain on governments and money markets. The old international system of linking currency to gold sputtered, was re-sparked, and then creaked along both at home and around the globe. The crash and collapse laid bare systemic monetary problems. The Depression was like the tide suddenly receding to reveal who had been swimming naked. In Canada's case, it was the banks.

The Depression led the Royal Bank, like all others, to protect itself from being stuck with defaults by calling in demand notes and tightening lending rules to people and businesses. It made sense to do so. Its loans on record went from $641 million in 1929 to only $385 million in 1933. However, in drying up the money to protect themselves the banks made bad problems worse.

In 1931, after years of discussions at international conferences, Britain announced that to address its monetary challenges it was abandoning the gold standard. From that point on, the country would print as much money as needed regardless of the amount of gold it had to back the notes. The Americans pledged to do the same. Because Canada's economy was so closely tied to both, Bennett had no real option but to let Canada's currency also float independently of gold. That decision, and related government actions, put more dollars into Canada's economy, but because of the chartered banks' monetary power, the federal government could only do so much when so much more was needed. Something big had to change.

Britain had created a central bank in 1694 after stealing the idea from the Dutch. The Americans created their central bank, the Federal Reserve, in 1913. After a year of careful consultation with bank directors who fought him and academics and economists who encouraged him, Bennett announced a Royal Commission to explore the creation of a Canadian central bank. Predictably, the banks attacked the idea. Their arguments about government having too much control over currency, however, held little sway amid loans being denied or called in, farms being taken, and houses foreclosed on. Banks and bankers had never been more unpopular. American bank robbers were folk heroes. A popular joke had a farmer's daughter becoming pregnant by a banker but the father forbidding a face-saving marriage saying he would rather shoulder the shame of a fatherless child in the family than a banker.

Most premiers stayed out of Bennett's fight with the banks, but some weighed in. Quebec's Louis-Alexandre Taschereau, for instance, had a letter published in the *Montreal Gazette* arguing that a national bank would place far too much power with the federal government and lead ultimately to Canada's destruction. Through its Canadian Bankers Association, the banks claimed the same.

Bennett stood firm. His position was afforded heft when the Royal Commission recommended the creation of a central bank. The bill creating the Bank of Canada was criticized in its details, but its necessity was supported by all three opposition parties. It received Royal Assent in July 1934.

Appointments needed to be made, new laws passed, and others amended to put the bank into operation. By 1944, Bank of Montreal $5 bills and all chartered bank currency were gathered up and turned into museum artifacts, since the banks could no longer, quite literally, print money. The banks fought especially hard to protect their gold. They demanded not just market value but to be further compensated if its value rose in the future. Bennett again stood firm and got the gold on terms that fairly benefited Canadians and not the banks' avarice.

The Bank of Canada opened its doors in March 1935. Operating independently of the banks and political pressure, it assumed control of monetary policy, including the manufacture and distribution of currency and the manipulation of the amount of money in the economy through a number of means, including interest rate fluctuations. Bennett said the bank was "a powerful instrument of social justice because it will be the means of insuring a greater measure of equity in the dealings of class with class; because it will be an independent source of advice and assistance in all matters relating to finance; because it begins a new chapter in the history of Canada's financial life."[3]

Many of those who later struggled to determine the causes of the Depression agreed with American economist Milton Friedman that had monetary issues been addressed sooner and better, it would not have been as deep or long. Certainly, Canada's economic stability was helped and later downturns avoided or mitigated because of actions taken by the Bank of Canada, yet another creation by a strong national government and strong national leader acting in the national interest.

The Americans sold the air. In the 1920s, radio was a new technological marvel. Wireless radio was shrinking space and time and linking people in ways never before believed conceivable. Entrepreneurs built radio stations and then networks to broadcast news, music, and, of course, advertising. In 1926, the U.S. government created the Federal Radio Commission. It established that the public owned the airwaves and outlined regulations and a licensing system that allowed broadcasters to use them.

As with other issues, Canada suffered from too much geography and not enough money. There were far fewer radio broadcasters in Canada and hardly any that reached remote areas. Meanwhile, American networks and lone-wolf stations grew quickly, with the air ignoring the ground's imaginary border. Canadians were entranced by radio, but most lived a hundred miles from the United States and heard nearly nothing but American programs and news.

In reaction to the waves of American voices and to pressure from the Catholic Church, which was angry about too many anti-Christian and anti-Catholic messages wafting into too many homes, Prime Minister King established a Royal Commission. The 1929 Aird Report said that some radio stations should be purchased, then owned and operated by the federal government. Like the publicly owned radio networks in Western Europe and Britain, a Canadian Crown corporation could foster a national spirit and interpret and enhance Canada's nationhood.

The Aird Report gathered dust while American radio networks built more stations and more powerful signals. In late 1929, the National Broadcasting Corporation (NBC) and the Columbia Broadcasting System (CBS) both announced plans to establish stations in Canada to send 100 percent American content to even more Canadians. First World War hero General Sir Arthur Currie, future Prime Minister Louis St. Laurent, our first female senator Cairine Wilson, and other concerned and powerful Canadians formed the National Council of the Canadian Radio League. Gathering support from a number of sectors, including banks, unions, and universities, the well-connected group demanded federal action on the Aird Report. With Bennett's election in 1930, they found their champion.

Despite the Aird Report and National Council of the Canadian Radio League, opposition was swift and fierce when

Bennett announced he wished to investigate the establishment of a publicly owned radio network. Many newspaper publishers didn't like radio in the first place because it was stealing advertising dollars from them, but they attacked the idea of public radio as representing unwarranted government economic intervention in the marketplace. Canada's private radio broadcasters were even more incensed. The natural competitors recognized a common cause and enemy. They rallied a number of corporations that were always ready to fight any government power and economic influence to give money and support to create a consortium. Included among them were Quaker Oats, Imperial Tobacco, Massey-Harris, and Supertest Petroleum. The consortium published and distributed a 19-page pamphlet attacking public radio entitled *Radio Broadcasting Under Private Ownership*.

Then the provinces entered the fray. Quebec launched a case that ended up at the Supreme Court. It argued that Ottawa could not create a publicly owned radio network because the issuing of radio licences was a provincial responsibility. The federal government argued that radio was not specifically mentioned in the Constitution and so according to the residual clause it was within its constitutional power. Furthermore, it argued, in 1927 Canada had signed the International Radiotelegraph Convention along with 78 other countries. This meant that radio fell under the federal government's treaty-signing power. The Supreme Court sided with the federal government, but Quebec appealed to the Judicial Committee of the Privy Council. In a rare instance of the JCPC supporting Ottawa's power, the provincial case was rejected.

Provincial opposition then took another tack. Quebec said public radio should not be established because the government should not condone or subsidize any venture that would lead to its people being swamped by English-language content. Other provinces, meanwhile, argued that the federal government should not create a public radio network because it would flood the airwaves with French content.

Bennett understood that culture is the glue of any civil society. He argued that Canadian culture must be protected and allowed to grow. This belief led him to pass more stringent guidelines to control American influence in the burgeoning Canadian magazine industry. With specific reference to radio, he said in February 1932, "The enormous benefits of an adequate scheme of radio broadcasting controlled and operated by Canadians is abundantly plain. Properly employed, the radio can be made a most effective instrument in nation building, with an education value difficult to estimate."[4]

A House of Commons Special Committee on Radio Broadcasting reported the opposition to public radio from a number of provincial governments, corporations, and corporate interests, but advocated its creation. Bennett answered critics with the double bottom-line argument that had built Macdonald's railway, and in a larger sense, created and given purpose to the national government in the first place. He said that private broadcasters could never be expected to provide service to remote communities, but that all Canadians deserved the advantages of citizenship and those included modern communications. Furthermore, he contended that citizenship and national unity involved sharing the broad narrative of nationhood and so the stories Canadians told other Canadians about Canada through artistic endeavours were important and must be encouraged. With America so close, Bennett argued, Canada's culture needed the support that only the federal government could offer on a pan-Canadian level. As he told the House of Commons,

> Without such control, radio broadcasting can never become the great agency for the communication of matters of national concern and for the diffusion of national thought and ideals, and without such control it can never be the agency by which national consciousness may be fostered and sustained and national unity still further strengthened.[5]

In May 1932, federal legislation created the Canadian Radio Broadcasting Corporation (CRBC). The CRBC initially took over the Canadian National Railway radio facilities that it had used to broadcast three hours of content a day from stations in Montreal, Toronto, Winnipeg, and Red Deer, Alberta. More were built. The nation-building venture was rendered more sustainable with the 1936 Canadian Broadcasting Act that morphed the CRBC into the Canadian Broadcasting Corporation (CBC)/Radio-Canada. The Crown corporation's mandate was made clearer and through government grants and licensing fees, its funding was rendered more stable.

We began hearing Canadian news and Canadian music and radio plays. The most popular program quickly became *Hockey Night in Canada*. In Saskatchewan farm kitchens, New Brunswick fishing villages, and Ontario tenement houses, we tuned in together to hear Foster Hewitt yell, "He shoots, he scores!" as we cheered our favourite players. As with friends and families, national connections grow deeper with shared moments. The national government was not through with using the air to build the nation.

❖

It had only been a generation since the Wright Brothers' Flyer skimmed the sand at Kitty Hawk, North Carolina. It was less than that since planes added a new dimension to warfare and only 10 years since brave bush pilots began taking supplies and critical medical help to remote northern communities. But by the mid-1930s, Canada was the world's only developed country whose major cities were not linked by air service. This void was enticing American air carriers to move north. There was money to be made, sovereignty to be protected, and another nuanced contribution to nationhood to be established.

A meeting was held in Ottawa. The minister of national defence, whose department at that point controlled aviation in Canada, and the postmaster general, who was concerned with the efficient movement of mail and delighted at the prospect of new opportunities and revenues, met with Clarence Decatur Howe. C.D. Howe was perhaps the most powerful cabinet minister in Canada's history. He was born in the United States but at 22 moved to Halifax to teach engineering at Dalhousie University. He then left academia for Ottawa's civil service. King was apprised of his intelligence and ambition, persuaded him to enter politics, and in 1935, Howe became the member of Parliament for Port Arthur, Ontario. He was appointed minister of marine, railways, and canals, and it was in this capacity that he chaired the Ottawa meeting. It was decided that Howe would recommend that his responsibilities be expanded to control civil aviation under a new department of transport.

Howe immersed himself in learning all he could about civil **aviation by consulting with British and American business** people and government officials. He also spoke repeatedly with Canadian business people and groups, including the presidents of Canadian National Railways (CNR) and Canadian Pacific Railway (CPR), who sought benefit from any new initiative. In 1930, the two railways had funded the creation of Canadian Airways to carry freight and mail. The combination of the Depression and federal government cuts to rail subsidies left Canadian Airways weak and underdeveloped. Howe concluded that, as in Britain and the United States, strong federal regulation of civil aviation was essential to ensure that destructive market competition and a concern only with profit would not limit mail and freight delivery or restrict passenger service to all but large urban centres.

So Howe announced a bill allowing the federal government to create a new company: Trans-Canada Air Lines (TCA). He negotiated with both railway companies, but in the end the CNR subscribed for all TCA shares, and its president, S.J. Hungerford, added the presidency of TCA to his job description. Howe made the final decision on the purchase of the company's first planes and then personally chose three men from his department to sit on the TCA board. The minister also interviewed Philip Johnson who had been president of Boeing and United Airlines. It took Howe only a couple of phone calls for Johnson to be appointed TCA's vice-president of operations.

Trans-Canada Air Lines didn't start from nothing, but almost. A few rudimentary airfields had been constructed in the 1920s and 1930s, but there were no air traffic towers or controllers to staff them. Regulations and processes were quickly drawn up, including that the railway would handle all ticketing and that stewardesses had to be registered nurses.

Despite growing pains, TCA developed quickly and efficiently. Howe directed the passage and implementation of the Transport Act. It created a board that oversaw the air transportation of mail, goods, and people. It licensed routes and ensured that TCA had a monopoly on transcontinental flights. Its regulations did not set prices, but policed them to ensure fairness. Beyond this, the Air Service branch of the Ministry of Transport assumed responsibility for the building and regulation of airports. The first TCA passenger flight took off from Montreal on April 1, 1939, and, after seven stopover landings, reached Vancouver only 18 hours later.

Trans-Canada Air Lines planes took to the air only 54 years after Sir John had celebrated Lord Strathcona's driving of the Canadian Pacific Railway's last spike at Craigellachie, British Columbia. The airline was the next logical step in Sir John's dream of establishing a transcontinental country and his determination to use the federal government's power to make it so.

While the nation-building creation of the Bank of Canada, CBC, and Trans-Canada Air Lines were being realized, the Depression's hurricane of destruction was easing but still ravaging businesses, farms, and families. There were pockets of prosperity that survived a temporary period of recovery, but employment generally remained as high as hopes were low. Too many roaming single young men still inhabited what were appropriately called jungles. Too many homeless and wandering souls warmed themselves beneath old newspapers night after bleak night. Fewer people were having children, or getting married, or for that matter could afford to get divorced.

As more people became more desperate, there was more crime. The need for more policing came just as municipal and provincial revenues were shrinking. Before Confederation, policing was a municipal responsibility and constabularies were created based on models imported from England and Ireland. The BNA Act established policing as a provincial responsibility. While cities kept their local departments, provincial departments were created to enforce provincial laws and offer policing to small communities and rural areas. Manitoba and Quebec formed their provincial police forces in 1870, British Columbia in 1872, Ontario in 1909, Saskatchewan and Alberta in 1917, New Brunswick in 1927, and Nova Scotia a year later.

The federal government had created the North-West Mounted Police (NWMP) in 1873 to administer and secure a Canadian presence in the country's recently acquired territories. Officers adopted red tunics to overtly borrow the legitimacy of the British Army. The NWMP helped move against the Métis in Saskatchewan and Native nations across the Prairies in the federal government's determined effort to establish sovereignty and its unique and tragic interpretation of order. It was also the NWMP that brought a semblance of stability to the chaos of the Yukon Gold Rush. Its strictly enforced rules saved lives by protecting prospectors from their blind enthusiasm. The national police also asserted Canadian sovereignty in the High Arctic when, in 1903, it established a post at Fort McPherson and another at Hudson Bay's Cape Fullerton. In 1904, the NWMP was renamed the Royal North-West Mounted Police (RNWMP).

In 1919, the federal government proposed merging the RNWMP with the Dominion Police, which had been responsible for guarding national buildings. Legislation was passed in November of that year, folding remnants of both into a new force called the Royal Canadian Mounted Police (RCMP) to enforce national laws that mostly dealt with narcotics and Aboriginal peoples while also offering national security. It would also do intelligence work, which really meant flushing Communists from labour unions and other areas of civil society.

While the RCMP's proposed mandate was limited, it still inspired opposition from many who believed it would be a federal intrusion into provincial jurisdiction. Maritime opposition was most vehement. Cape Breton South MP Robert Butts reflected Maritime fears when he exclaimed in the House, "We never had need of the Mounted Police down there and we have no need of them now … do not send hayseeds from away across the plains down to Nova Scotia. I say it is dangerous to send them there. I speak for 73,000 people from Cape Breton and I can say they will not appreciate such an intrusion."[6] Provincial opposition was considered, but the RCMP was nonetheless formed in February 1920. Promises were made to stay out of provincial police operations and jurisdictions.

Just as it seemed as if policing was working itself out, the provinces faced difficult decisions. Saskatchewan was first. It had assumed control of policing from the RNWMP in January 1917 to form the Saskatchewan Provincial Police (SPP). Commissioner Charles Mahoney had hired and trained officers mostly from among returning soldiers and the province's RNWMP detachment. The SPP chased bank robbers, thieves, and cattle rustlers and handled domestic violence, bar fights, and myriad other criminals and insanity that keeps police busy everywhere.

Only nine years later, the Saskatchewan government felt the financial burden of running its own provincial police force. It was calculated that the SPP cost $500 million a year while the RCMP could do the same work for less than half, or about $200 million. Some said to forget the money because the province had a constitutional responsibility to provide policing and having the federal government do the job would be a surrender of provincial sovereignty. Money won the day. The application was made, the RCMP accepted, and in 1928 Saskatchewan's provincial police was disbanded.

The Depression brought Saskatchewan policing arguments to other provinces. Municipalities having trouble meeting police budgets sought help from their provincial capitals. Provincial governments watched crime rates increase while their ability to help declined. Crushing fiscal pressures blurred memories of fighting the feds, and the provinces turned to Ottawa.

Prime Minister Bennett offered RCMP service to all provinces at the cost of $1,000 per officer. This was significantly lower than the provinces' police costs. Alberta's provincial police, for example, cost $1,680 per officer. As had happened in Saskatchewan, sovereignty argued with solvency. British Columbia, Ontario, and Quebec said no. New Brunswick, Prince Edward Island, Nova Scotia, Alberta, and Manitoba, however, took the deal. They all disbanded provincial police forces that they could simply no longer afford and accepted the Canadian police. British Columbia would retire its provincial police in 1950.

The RCMP grew. Many of the new officers were absorbed from the disbanded provincial forces. It became a more professional organization with Commissioner Major-General Sir James MacBrien implementing national standards. He insisted upon more rigorous recruitment and training protocols, better communication methods, and more and better equipment. Vehicles, airplanes, and high-speed boats were purchased. New technology was adopted, such as the RCMP forensic laboratory in Regina. The provinces could not have made all the advances in technology and service to Canadians on their own.

The combination of too many unemployed young men, the RCMP's new power, and provincial inability to meet constitutional responsibilities led to tragic consequences in 1935. It began in British Columbia. Since striking a hard bargain to join Canada, successive B.C. premiers had used the residual feeling of Canada needing it more than it needed Canada to push for concessions. There was great consternation when the federal government disallowed several of its anti-Chinese laws that were as blatantly ultra vires as they were racist. It was pressure from British Columbia that led Ottawa to impose a $500 head tax (an astronomical sum at the time) on Chinese immigrants. In 1906, British Columbia even won a 10-year $100,000 annual payment from Ottawa to redress what it argued was unfair advantages in the federal government's ability to raise revenues. Eastern papers dubbed British Columbia the "spoiled child of Confederation."

Farmers, fishers, miners, and timber workers were especially hard hit by the Depression, and British Columbia had plenty of all four. Provincial resource revenue fell by 48 percent. Debt added to the province's dilemma. Like other provinces, British Columbia had borrowed heavily to finance infrastructure development in the heady 1920s. By 1933, the banks and bond markets declared British Columbia's **credit exhausted.**

Economic devastation on the Prairies brought thousands of migrant workers to where prospects were a little better and winters a lot warmer. Thomas Dufferin Pattullo (everyone called him Duff) became B.C. premier in November 1933. When he was opposition leader, he had decried provincial projects that put unemployed young men to work building roads and bridges. He had also criticized the province's building of camps to house men for remote work. As premier, however, he swung quickly to support the projects and camps and argue for their expansion. But he found the cupboard bare. British Columbia needed help. It needed Ottawa.

In 1931, Prime Minister Bennett's minister of labour, Gideon Robertson, reported that during a recent tour of British Columbia and Alberta he had sensed simmering violence among thousands of unemployed young men. He recommended an increased RCMP and army presence in a number of western cities and the construction of relief camps to house and employ the young men. Bennett consulted broadly, including with Pattullo, and in the fall of 1932 he put the Department of National Defence in charge of constructing relief camps.

The first of 237 camps were built in Alberta and British Columbia. They were soon in remote areas of many provinces and filled with men who voluntarily enrolled. The men were not given wages, but they did receive $20 a day in spending money, a cigarette ration, and free food and shelter. They cleared trees and built fences, roads, bridges, and airstrips. By the time the camps were closed in 1936, more than 170,000 young men had spent time in them.

British Columbia still operated its own relief camps and so the province had two camp systems. Pattullo welcomed the new camps and began withdrawing funding and support for his own. By 1933, men started protesting camp conditions deemed harsh and rules declared draconian. Pattullo began receiving letters and delegations and wrote to Bennett explaining that a number of men had been thrown out for stirring unrest. He implored the prime minister to let them back in and to address complaints.

American-born Arthur "Slim" Evans, a Communist, led the Relief Camp Workers' Union. In December 1934, with 500 relief workers chanting outside the Victoria legislature, Evans presented Pattullo with a 30,665-signature petition demanding better work conditions and better pay. Pattullo wrote more letters to Bennett. One asked the prime minister to close the camps. Another said conditions must be improved and still another demanded that the protesters and other unemployed men be arrested and imprisoned.

Relief camp troubles boiled over in April 1935 when 1,500 strikers left their B.C. camps and converged on Vancouver. Mayor Gerry McGeer quite literally read the riot act to protesters in Victory Square. They laughed. McGeer informed the premier that he could no longer handle the situation. Hearing unsatisfactory ideas from Pattullo, the mayor wired increasingly alarmist appeals to Bennett. Meanwhile, Bennett was receiving equally desperate demands for Ottawa's intervention from Pattullo. The prime minister expressed concern regarding the constitutional ramifications of the federal government sending the RCMP or army to address the situation. The premier forgot all the constitutional fights and demands for greater independence that his province had waged for decades and insisted on immediate federal action.

On June 3, 1,000 strikers implemented a new idea and set off by train to take their case to Ottawa. The On to Ottawa

Trek was born. Their numbers grew with each mile east. At each city and town in which they stopped, mayors and premiers did all they could to keep the peace and keep them moving. Convinced the trek was a Communist plot to disrupt the rule of law, Bennett ordered the RCMP to stop it in Regina. Saskatchewan Premier Jimmy Gardiner was outraged. He wrote to express support for Bennett's interpretation of the trek and strikers and agreement that it needed to be halted before reaching Ottawa, but demanded that it be allowed to first get through his province.

Word leaked and everyone knew the trek would hit the Regina roadblock. A last-minute meeting with the strike leaders took place with Bennett, but solved nothing. On a warm July evening, about 500 strikers and 1,000 onlookers were listening to a speech in Regina's Market Square. Three unmarked vans took up positions. With the shrieking blast of a whistle, the van doors were flung open and bat-wielding RCMP officers poured into the crowd. There were screams and blood and broken bones. The roiling riot spilled into neighbouring streets. The next morning more than 100 strikers were in jail, 30 were in hospital, and Constable Charles Millar was dead. The strike was over. The trek was over. Most strikers accepted Ottawa's offer of free rail tickets back to their camps.

A Royal Commission determined that the existence of provincial and federal government camps in British Columbia had created confusion over different camp conditions but that camp life was generally good and as advertised. The majority of men were satisfied with the rules and the opportunity to work. A commission investigating the Regina Riot found that local and provincial officials could have done more to handle the situation before it spun out of control, but it exonerated the Bennett government. It concluded that Ottawa had acted according to the law and Constitution. Both the Royal Commission and the Regina Riot Inquiry Commission supported the statement that Bennett had made just five days after the riot and that foreshadowed Prime Minister Pierre Trudeau's remarks during the 1970 FLQ Crisis: "It is not the intention of this Government to allow such demonstrations as will interfere with the maintenance of law and order throughout the country."[7]

Despite the fact that premiers, especially Pattullo, had demanded that Ottawa act, they were quick to criticize the action when it came. The blood on the Regina streets was washed away, but, as in Winnipeg in 1919, another police riot stained Canada's history. It is a reminder of the necessity of the federal government to act decisively in the face of provincial unwillingness or inability to handle situations, but also the need to defuse rather than inflame.

By the end of Bennett's tenure, unemployment remained monstrously high in some regions but was lower than at its peak two years earlier. Throughout his long political career and certainly throughout his term as prime minister, R.B. Bennett was on the left of his party and what would later be called a Progressive Conservative or Red Tory. He believed in using the power of the federal government to bring stability to our national economy while creating more equal opportunities for all. In January 1935, with a federal election on the horizon, Bennett personally paid for five radio spots to announce a series of proposals. He declared laissez-faire capitalism dead. To create a more stable and fairer economic structure, he proposed more intervention through the creation of new or augmented programs involving unemployment insurance, old-age security, pensions, and health care. He proposed stricter regulation of banks and financial institutions.

Canadians were shocked less by the ideas, many of which he had been talking about for years, than the strident tone. Bennett commenced turning the ideas into law. The October 1935 election, however, offered Canadians a chance to express their rage at a government that had been unable to end the Depression. Western provinces offered new party alternatives with the Co-operative Commonwealth Federation, Social Credit, and even breakaway Conservatives in the Reconstruction Party. The split votes and anti-Bennett anger put King back in the prime minister's office.

Although he had campaigned against Bennett's interventionist policies and programs, King kept nearly all of them. Most significantly, in November 1935, he referred all of what had been dubbed Bennett's "New Deal" legislation to the Supreme Court. It made sense. Bennett's Minimum Wages Act, Employment and Social Insurance Act, Natural Products Marketing Act, Farmers' Credit Arrangement Act, and Hours of Work Act were all bold national laws and programs, but all intruded on provincial jurisdiction. Bennett was a skilled lawyer who had argued to his cabinet that the Depression constituted a national emergency and so the Peace, Order, and Good Government clause validated Ottawa's actions.

Respected Ontario Chief Justice Newton Rowell and Quebec constitutional lawyer Louis St. Laurent expertly argued Ottawa's case. But they lost. The Supreme Court sided with the provinces and declared every law unconstitutional. This time it was the federal government that appealed to the Judicial Committee of the Privy Council. In January 1937, the JCPC said the Depression did not meet the standard of a national emergency, and so, with the exception of the Farmers' Credit Arrangement Act, declared every "New Deal" law unconstitutional.

Despite the ruling, it remained clear to dispassionate observers that national programs of the nature Bennett had introduced were necessary for the good of Canada and Canadians. It was equally clear that the programs could never be implemented unless the federal government's power that Sir John and the founders envisioned could escape the straitjacket in which the JCPC had placed it. Furthermore, progress was impossible unless new fiscal arrangements could be negotiated to allow provinces to meet their constitutional obligations. It was with these thoughts in mind that King's government created the Royal Commission on Dominion-Provincial Relations. It was to investigate and report on "legislative powers essential to a proper carrying out of the federal system in harmony with national needs and the promotion of national unity." Dubbed the Rowell-Sirois Commission, it worked for three years and visited every province. Fearing an intrusion into provincial jurisdictions, the Alberta and Quebec governments refused to co-operate.

The commission's conclusions were stunning. The report was in accord with what Bennett had argued and the Depression had proved: the overlapping federal and provincial tax systems were a mess and provincial fiscal capabilities hampered their meeting constitutional responsibilities. Affording provinces more revenue-generating power could solve the problem, but the vast difference in wealth and potential between regions and provinces would render that solution unfair to too many Canadians. A national solution was needed for the national problem. The commissioners said that Ottawa should be given more power to raise revenue within a system that more explicitly demarcated sources of national and provincial taxation. With its additional money, Ottawa should establish unconditional "National Adjustment Grants" and send the funds to provincial governments according to a formula that calculated financial need. The grants would mitigate provincial and regional economic disparities. To further help Canadians by helping the provinces, it recommended a program of national unemployment insurance similar to that created by Bennett but shot down by the JCPC. Finally, it advised that the federal government do as it had done when welcoming new provinces to Canada and assume their debts. In short, the commission advocated Sir John's vision of a stable federal system led by a powerful central government while acknowledging the legitimacy of the decades-long struggle for strong provinces. The federal government declared support for the recommendations and the vision upon which they were based. A number of premiers, on the other hand, began attacking both because while the implementation of the recommendations could benefit Canada as a whole, those benefits would not immediately accrue to their provinces.

King convened a federal-provincial conference to discuss it all. The January 1941 conference fell into predictable camps. Quebec argued that accepting the report would result in the surrender of too much power to the federal government and the provinces becoming only "phantoms" with "enslaved people" unable to fend for themselves. Quebec would be less able to protect its unique interests. The other rich provinces — Alberta, Ontario, and British Columbia — were just as vehement in their rejection of the proposals. Ontario Premier Mitchell Hepburn derided the report's cost, ridiculed its authors, and called those who supported its recommendations "enemies of civilization." Nova Scotia's premier wryly observed that the provinces arguing against the report were those who would not receive National Adjustment Grants. On the other hand, Manitoba and Saskatchewan had nearly declared bankruptcy during the Depression. They and the Maritime provinces would receive grants, and perhaps not surprisingly, all liked the idea.

The conference ended in an indecisive shambles. However, the report's illustrating the provinces' fiscal capacity versus their constitutional responsibility highlighted a significant problem that resonated with enough level heads that at least one recommendation was implemented. A constitutional amendment was passed that allowed the federal government to create a national program of unemployment insurance. Provinces were quick to surrender that sliver of power for not again having to pay relief. Beginning in the summer of 1941, Canadians paid a portion of their salaries into a federal fund from which they could draw if their jobs suddenly vanished. But these changes to Ottawa's power were taking place when most people were directing their attention elsewhere. The world had again caught fire.

4

WAR AGAIN

Prime Minister William Lyon Mackenzie King looked deeply into Adolf Hitler's eyes. He liked what he saw. The Führer's foreign minister, Joachim von Ribbentrop, had set up their meeting. Ribbentrop knew Canada well after having run a wine business in Ottawa and Montreal before returning home for the First World War. Hitler welcomed the prime minister to Germany's opulent Hindenburg Palace on June 29, 1937. Instead of his Nazi uniform, Hitler was dressed in a statesman's dark suit. For more than an hour, they discussed Canada, Germany, world events, and the ominous threat of war.

Hitler had been in power for four years, and in a clear violation of the Versailles Treaty's terms, was rapidly rebuilding Germany's military. He had already begun territorial conquests. He was already implementing the Holocaust's first horrendous stages. King told Hitler that his power came from the people and Canadians did not want war. However, he warned, should a European war begin, and should Britain become involved, Canada would fight at its side.

Hitler spoke of peace. Warm handshakes and an exchange of gifts ended their cordial meeting. The prime minister presented a book, and Hitler, ever the narcissist, offered a framed, signed photograph of himself. King later dictated a long diary entry in which he confessed to being impressed by the Nazi leader. He found him "a calm, passive man, deeply and thoughtfully earnest … one could see, how particularly humble folk would come to have a profound love for the man…. As I talked with him, I could not but think of Joan of Arc. He is distinctly mystic."[1]

Winston Churchill did not meet Hitler. But he was not fooled. While adrift in the political wilderness, Churchill raged at Britain's unwillingness to recognize evil and act against it. Finally, though, with the invasion of Poland on September 1, 1939, there was no one left to fool. Two days later Britain declared war.

Canada's government, without the advice of the premiers, had a momentous decision to make. The Statute of Westminster meant that, unlike in 1914, Britain's declaration of war presented Canada with no obligation to follow suit. However, the Canadian link to Britain remained strong. Its strength had been revealed in the joyous reception enjoyed by King George VI and Queen Elizabeth on their spring cross-Canada tour only months before. The British monarch greeted so many people that a doctor examined his swollen and aching right hand and suggested he switch to shaking hands with his left. Always a keen observer of public opinion, Prime Minister King had proudly escorted the Royal Couple and noted the size of the crowds and spontaneity of the cheers, even in Quebec. Despite Canadians' reaction to the Royal Visit, King knew the first global war in support of Britain had torn Canada's unity, with Quebec nationalists fighting British imperialists. He worried that another war would restart the rending.

King consulted his cabinet, which expressed support for the war. As with all issues, he paid special attention to Ernest Lapointe. Lapointe was King's minister of justice, his most trusted adviser, and his Quebec lieutenant. He told the prime minister that Quebecers' fear of conscription was informing their negative reaction to the new European war.

The prime minister rose in the House a few days later and stated that regardless of the costs and threats to national unity, Canada needed to declare war to defend the country and stand by Britain. He said that Hitler's territorial desires could very well include Canada because of its great resource wealth. He promised that there would be no conscription for soldiers to be sent overseas, but that there very well might be a need to draft men for home defence. He summarized his talk with a statement that was short on Churchillian eloquence but was rousing nonetheless — the voice of a national leader inspiring a national effort as only a national leader can:

> We stand for the defence of Canada; we stand for the co-operation of this country at the side of Great Britain … let no hasty or premature threat or pronouncement create mistrust and divisions between the different elements that compose the population of our vast dominion, so that when the moment of decision came all should so see the issue itself that our national effort might be marked by unity of purpose, of heart and of endeavour.[2]

Three days later, a week after the British declaration, due almost entirely to its ancestral and familial British ties, and despite concern over a Quebec backlash, Canada declared war.

Canadians were quick to respond. Across the country, including in Quebec, they lined up to fight. Forms, procedures, uniforms, barracks, and everything else needed to accept the waves of volunteers were quickly and sometimes inefficiently hammered together. No one bought the old pitch of war's glory as they had in 1914, but the dedication to duty was just as fervent. A strong assertion of united purpose led Canadians to a great moral fight that, unlike the first time, needed to be fought.

Before battling Nazis, however, King had to fight premiers. Quebec Premier Maurice Duplessis was a brilliant politician who had been working carefully with powerful Catholic Church leaders while keeping nationalists at bay and all the while bringing progress to a province that was slowly and begrudgingly shedding its agrarian sensibilities. He had allied himself with Ontario's Mitchell Hepburn in 1937 to fight what he saw as the Rowell-Sirois Report's attempt to diminish provincial power. He and Hepburn argued that Confederation was nothing more than a treaty between the provinces. That meant the federal government was a child of the provinces and, like all children, should be quiet and obedient. It was he and Hepburn who were paramount in preventing King's ability to do much that the report had recommended. The war with Hitler made their war with Ottawa more intense. Duplessis insisted that Ottawa was doing too much in putting the country on a war footing and Hepburn said it was doing too little. Both acted in what they believed were the best interests of their provinces, but they clearly placed partisan and parochial concerns above the interests and needs of the country, not to mention those being crushed beneath Nazi jackboots.

Maurice Duplessis acted first. Elected Quebec's Conservative Party leader in 1933, two years later Duplessis had formed an alliance of opposition parties under the banner Union Nationale. In August 1936, his new party formed the government. He demonstrated his willingness to work with Ottawa when it suited his purposes, such as when he tied Quebec to the national old-age pension program. Duplessis also happily accepted Ottawa's money for make-work projects. However, he was quick to attack the federal government when the war threatened to affect Quebec.

In May 1939, Duplessis had spoken kindly to and about the Royal Couple during their Quebec stay, but four months later he railed against participation in a "foreign war" being fought for nothing more than "antiquated" British ties. His antipathy to the war and the federal government were married to his revulsion over Prime Minister King's invocation of the War Measures Act. As in the First World War, the act allowed cabinet to issue orders-in-council deemed necessary to meet the emergency. Duplessis argued that orders-in-council and the War Measures Act itself were undemocratic. His accusation was more than a little precious given that only two years before, his government had passed the Padlock Laws, which allowed Quebec's provincial police to ignore citizenship rights in arresting those deemed enemies of the state. But now Duplessis stated that the War Measures Act was a vehicle through which King might break his conscription promise while intruding into the provincial sphere of power. Duplessis was also upset with the federal government for the Bank of Canada's refusal to grant a loan to his government that was needed because, due to the United States Neutrality Act, Quebec could no longer borrow in American markets. Neither were King's doing, of course, but in politics, perception often matters more than the truth and capturing a narrative can advance agendas. In speeches and media interviews, Duplessis focused blame for his province's problems and the potential for more squarely on Ottawa.

Just two weeks after Canada's declaration of war, and two years before the end of his current mandate, Duplessis called an election. He said it was necessary to stand up for Quebec's rights and fight Ottawa and the threat of conscription for the good of Quebecers. King needed to react. He was doing all he could to limit Canada's involvement in the war. But Canada's ability to meet its domestic and international obligations could be compromised if Duplessis succeeded in blaming the federal government for Quebec's ills and turning Quebecers and possibly others against Ottawa and the war. King confided to his diary: "It is a diabolical act on his part to have made the issue provincial autonomy versus the Dominion Government to have it appear that Ottawa is encroaching on freedom of individuals in Quebec. No doubt he and Hepburn had intended to make provincial autonomy the issue … the Quebec-Ontario axis will be smashed."[3]

King's most important Quebec ministers agreed. Ernest Lapointe called Duplessis's words and actions "sabotage" and "unpatriotic." Lapointe, Arthur Cardin, and Chubby Power consulted with cabinet and then left to actively campaign to defeat Duplessis. In speeches on the radio and in church basements, Legion halls, and school gyms, they attacked the Union Nationale leader for playing politics while people's lives were at risk and the Western world was besieged. They said it was never constructive to attack the federal government to gain greater provincial autonomy, and in wartime it was unpatriotic. They told Quebecers that if Duplessis was returned to power, they would resign from cabinet. No Quebecers would be left at the decision-making table to fight for Quebec, and possibly, against conscription.

The political momentum spun so fast that Duplessis was knocked off balance. He stumbled, reacted, and never regained the narrative. The October 25 election saw the provincial Liberals crush Duplessis by winning 70 seats to the Union Nationale's 15. The victory was the federal government's. It saluted the notion that there are times when demeaning a national effort in a scrap for provincial power is simply inappropriate.

With the recalcitrant premier removed, King was able to more fully focus on building Canada's military and supporting Britain. King had boosted the military budget in 1935 when it was increasingly clear that European tensions were becoming more acute. With the Nazi war machine presenting the greatest fighting force yet assembled, King was reminded that Canada's defence budget was woefully insufficient. The Royal Canadian Air Force (RCAF) had nearly 300 officers and 3,000 airmen, and it boasted 270 aircraft, but only 37 were ready for service. The Royal Canadian Navy (RCN) had only 2,000 officers and men and six ocean-going vessels, two of which should have been decommissioned years before. The Canadian Army had just a few big guns, two tanks, and just over 4,000 men. King was informed that the country had only three small arms-manufacturing plants. That was it. If Canada was to meet its obligations, the federal government would need to take the lead and start nearly from scratch.

The budget for all three military services in 1939–40 was substantially up from just a few years before, but still only $64.6 million. The chiefs of staff told cabinet that at least $491 million would be needed to train, equip, and send the three divisions that Britain requested. Cabinet cut it to $314 million and the number of divisions that would make up the expeditionary force from three to one.

In the war's first month, the army enlisted nearly 60,000 young men. The problem was not gathering the civilian soldiers but supplying them with uniforms, barracks, shipping, weapons, and everything else needed to create an armed force. To get the supply rolling to meet the overwhelming demand, King appointed Wallace Campbell, the president of Ford Motor Company of Canada, to head the newly constituted War Supply Board. It was quickly evident that Wallace, the board's mandate, and its budget were inadequate to the task, In November, King created a powerful new ministry called Munitions and Supply. C.D. Howe, the minister of transport who had shown such élan in the formation of Trans-Canada Air Lines, was asked to add this new ministry to his responsibilities.

Howe attacked the challenge with unbridled passion and ruthless efficiency. It involved a national effort and nothing short of readjusting the power of government and its relationship with corporate, business, and financial interests, and with citizens. He would need to consider the always wary and often prickly provinces. Howe somehow had to also rally Canada's capacity to meet orders for armaments not yet received and pay for it all with money from God knows where. He was the perfect man for the job.

Before Howe could really begin his work, however, another provincial premier threw obstacles before him and Canada's war effort. Ontario's Mitchell Hepburn was a mercurial, hard-drinking, hard-partying man who offended many but charmed all. As an impetuous 30-year-old, he had been elected to the House of Commons and had impressed King with his wit and work ethic. Only four years later, he won the leadership of the Ontario Liberals and then, after one of the dirtiest campaigns the province had ever seen, became its youngest premier. Hepburn's administration set a frenetic pace that strained his health without restraining his alcohol consumption, all-night parties, or number of sexual partners.

Hepburn was always willing to make or break alliances to suit immediate needs. His relationship with King was stretched during the hard-fought conference at which the federal government had struggled with the provinces over Rowell-Sirois recommendations. It frayed more when King asked and Hepburn refused to reverse a decision to close Ontario's old lieutenant governor's mansion and then when Hepburn asked but King refused to appoint his old agriculture minister to the Senate. The relationship snapped when King would not grant approval for Ontario to sell excess hydro-electric power to New York State. Hepburn made it clear that he was a Liberal but not a Mackenzie King Liberal. He then moved beyond the issues at hand by attacking the federal government's war effort. Hepburn told a reporter, "It would make you sick to see how confused and distraught everything and everyone is in Ottawa."[4] There was a showdown coming.

Over the Christmas holidays, with Europe slumped into the tense, quiet months of what was dubbed the Phony War, Hepburn plotted his attack. On January 18, 1940, he rose in the Ontario legislature and introduced a resolution offering regret that the federal government was letting Canadians down by failing to meet our war responsibilities in the vigorous manner that they and the cause deserved. His majority assured its passage.

A week after Hepburn's announcement, King visited the governor general and revealed his reaction. Lord Tweedsmuir gasped but acquiesced. On January 25, His Excellency read the Speech from the Throne to open Parliament's next session, but concluded by saying that the House was dissolved and the election would take place on March 26, 1940.

King and his colleagues met the country with the assertion that Hepburn was acting in a treasonous fashion and was as anti-Canadian as Duplessis had been. This was a time for unity of purpose, they said, not Ottawa bashing and petty bickering. Furthermore, King said there would be no coalition government such as that advocated by Hepburn and federal Conservative leader Robert Manion. Such a move, he argued, would be a step toward dictatorship. Finally, King repeated that while necessity might result in conscripting men for home service, conscripts would never fight overseas. King's Liberals won a bigger majority than they had enjoyed before and more than 50 percent of the national popular vote. Notably, King's Liberals also won over 50 percent of the popular vote in Ontario. A second premier was slammed and shamed by Canadians expressing their loyalty through the most reliable and powerful tool at their disposal — the ballot box. They said again that the federal government was their voice.

The federal government again got back to work. The task grew more immediate when, in the spring of 1940, the seven-month Phony War ended and country after country fell to the Nazi blitzkrieg. Minister of Munitions and Supply C.D. Howe began his military-like operation to create military-ready equipment by persuading prominent private-sector people to join him. More than a hundred "dollar-a-year men," who represented the cream of Canada's corporate lawyers, business leaders, and corporate elite, had salaries paid by their companies, and under federal government auspices, donated their time and talents for their country. Many coordinated orders and procurement. Others became controllers who oversaw production in various sectors such as timber, coal, and steel.

The need for a national effort, married to the powers of the War Time Supply Act and the War Measures Act, allowed Ottawa to bypass the ideological questions some business people might normally raise and constitutional roadblocks provinces might naturally erect. To build as much as could be built as quickly as possible, Howe oversaw the creation of 28 Crown corporations. They handled tasks as varied as importing and producing synthetic rubber to bringing specialized machine tools from the United States. Orders went out with grants and loans to private Canadian businesses and work began. Howe located the newly constituted Munitions and Supply Office in London to sidestep the Westminster bureaucracy and more directly and efficiently meet British needs.

Contracts and jobs were spread across the country and lingering Depression-era unemployment evaporated. Ottawa's National Selective Service system moved people to where the jobs were and there were few complaints from those happy to finally have work with as much overtime as they wanted. The government's wage-and-price control system kept salaries and inflation low, but wages rose steadily and outstripped slowly rising prices on goods and services. Temporary wartime housing was built for workers moved near suddenly thriving factories. While the American Rosie the Riveter over-glamorized women's role in defence production, the reality was that many urban women enjoyed their first jobs outside their homes. Before war's end, more than 261,000 Canadian women laboured in factories, with their contributions helping their families and the war effort while proving that strength, resolve, and patriotism are not gender-specific.

Howe called it a "bits and pieces" program. But all those bits and pieces were expensive. In 1939 alone, the federal government invested what at the time was an astronomical $3.65 billion. King and his cabinet ministers rallied the country to the cause and the country responded. Canadians lent the government $12.5 billion through their enthusiastic purchase of Victory Bonds. Canadian businesses bought Victory Bonds too, while also ponying up more taxes. Corporate rates jumped from 18 percent to 40 percent. Howe's team ensured generous depreciation allowances for companies that retooled, rebuilt, or expanded, but profits on government contracts were limited to 10 percent. The profit mongering that had marred the First World War would not be tolerated in this fight. Instead, as H.R. MacMillan of Howe's ministry boldly proclaimed to British Columbia lumbermen, there would be a "sharing of losses."

C.D. Howe became known as the minister of everything. Among the major initiatives he tackled was Canada's commitment to the British Commonwealth Air Training Plan (BCATP). Canada, Australia, New Zealand, and Britain had agreed that Canada would train pilots, navigators, and other air crew members and support staff. The federal government would be tested by the deadline that had training scheduled to begin only months later.

Howe split the country into four training commands. Staff were hired, plans made, and soon hundreds of communities still digging late-winter snow saw airfields and bases being built or expanded. Britain had agreed to provide the Anson aircraft for training purposes, but when it could not do so, Howe created another Crown corporation, appointed one of his men to lead it, and Canadian aircraft production began. Plus, before America's Neutrality Act took effect, 35 aircraft were purchased. Facing a shortage of male trainers, the RCAF Women's Division was pressed into service.

Seeing the bonanza of construction and spinoff jobs and growing tax revenue, as well as wanting to assist in the patriotic effort, premiers and mayors lobbied for bases in their jurisdictions. News of a new base was often celebrated with parties and parades, and more festivities welcomed the arrival of staff and then trainees. At picnics, sports days, and dances, a jumble of accents from trainers not much older than the trainees made for great fun and stories. But there was also sadness when crashes took those whom townsfolk had come to know. Air-training accidents stole the lives of 856 young men.

The BCATP cost more than King or Howe had predicted: a staggering $1.6 billion. But it was a roaring success. By the end of the war, there were 107 air-training schools involving nearly 11,000 aircraft. More than 131,000 men were trained. The program employed over 104,000 Canadians and helped build and bolster cities and towns at 231 locations around the country. More than half of all Commonwealth pilots were trained in Canada. U.S. President Roosevelt was not exaggerating when he called Canada the "aerodrome of democracy."

As the BCATP was being implemented, Howe also coordinated the production of raw materials and war *matériel*.

Canada punched far above its weight in providing $5.8 billion in copper, lead, asbestos, zinc, nickel, and more. It produced uranium used in America's atomic bomb research and development. Canada's production of weaponry and equipment was equally staggering. The federal effort organized the building of 16,400 aircraft, which included 15 giant Lancaster bombers a month. By the end of the war, 90 shipyards had built 410 merchant marine ships and 206 corvettes, as well as hundreds of frigates, Tribal class destroyers, and other classes of ships. For the army, Canadian factories turned out 2,000 Ram tanks that were later converted into armoured personnel carriers. It also built and shipped 815,729 trucks, ambulances, and other vehicles. Beyond all of that, Canadian workers fashioned shells, bullets, rockets, torpedoes, and a vast array of light and heavy guns and other weaponry.

While producing all of this and more, the Canadian navy and merchant seamen kept the North Atlantic sea lanes open to allow it all to get to Britain. Young men showed remarkable courage as they plied the roiling, freezing sea while at any moment U-boats could attack from below or aircraft from above.

But all this effort and courage was at risk because the money necessary to keep it all churning forward was running out and threatening to screech everything to a stop. What had happened in the First World War was happening again. Britain had reached a point where it had no currency left to lend or buy Canadian stuff, or to support Canada's efforts to support it. For all intents and purposes, Britain was broke. King was left with a quandary but only one real option. He would need to do as Robert Borden had done and turn to the United States. King had already met Roosevelt in August 1940 in FDR's private railway car in Ogdensburg, New York. Their discussions led to an agreement to coordinate the guarding of the continent through the creation of the Permanent Joint Board of Defence. This move was natural and necessary, given that the days were long gone when Canada could count on Britain's help to defend its coastlines and airspace.

The next spring saw FDR and Churchill agree to the Lend-Lease Act. Roosevelt explained that when a neighbour's house is on fire you don't dicker over the price of your garden hose, you simply give it happily and later worry about payment or replacement. In this case, the United States initially gave Britain some old American destroyers and other necessary weapons and aid in return for a promise to pay later and for the surrender of military bases, including in Newfoundland.

A problem with the Lend-Lease agreement was that in April 1941, a month after the U.S. Congress approved it, Britain began cancelling Canadian orders. Why pay for Canadian goods when American goods were free? At the same time, the third year of importing so much from the United States to keep Canadian factories humming had resulted in too many American dollars leaving the Canadian treasury. Canada's foreign exchange account was nearly drained.

Howe proposed a deal to the Americans, and King met Roosevelt at the president's Hyde Park estate to negotiate the details. Canada needed money and Britain needed war *matériel*. The United States could not produce enough to meet Britain's needs on its own. A solution to all three problems was found when the president and prime minister agreed that the United States would increase its defence orders in Canada by $200 to $300 million over the next year. Plus, American parts for products needed to fill British orders would be shipped to Canadian factories and the goods manufactured would become part of the Lend-Lease arrangement. The Hyde Park agreement ensured that the British-American Lend Lease would involve Canada and not crush it. Canada's trade deficit would shrink, a run on the dollar would be avoided, Canadians would be kept employed, and weapons and supplies would continue to flow to Britain and to Canadian troops.

Just over half, 53 percent of all Canadian war production, went to Britain and other Commonwealth countries. About 12 percent went to the United States, and Canadian forces used the rest. Ottawa spent $11 billion on the building of industrial capacity and wartime production. To approximate that amount into today's dollars, multiply the figure by 10. Winston Churchill praised Canada's wartime production and commitment to Britain and the war several times, including in a December 1941 speech in Canada's House of Commons in which he said, "The contribution of Canada to the Imperial war effort in troops, in ships, in aircraft, in food, and in finance, has been magnificent."[5] There is, in fact, a consensus among British historians that without Canada, Britain would not have survived 1940–41.[6]

Nazi victories in the spring of 1940 demonstrated that the war would be longer and tougher than anticipated and that an all-volunteer Canadian military might not be enough. The conscripting of citizens to become soldiers had damaged Canada in the First World War. King was determined that mistakes made then would not be repeated. Ottawa passed the National Resources Mobilization Act. It inaugurated the registration of all military-age men for possible home duty. The measure was accepted nearly everywhere and especially welcomed by families of those with members already serving.

Not everyone was happy, though. The most vocal opposition to the steps toward conscription came from Montreal Mayor Camillien Houde. Houde had sat in the provincial and federal legislatures, but he hit his stride as mayor from 1928 to 1932, and then again from 1934 to 1936, and yet again when re-elected in 1938. While claiming loyalty to Canada and Britain, he was a vocal supporter of Mussolini and Fascism. He urged the men of his city and, in fact, all Quebecers to ignore Ottawa's National Resources Mobilization Act. Houde told young men to refuse to register.

At first King ignored the Montreal mayor. However, when it became apparent that significant numbers of young Quebecers were heeding Houde's call to defy Canadian law, King decided that action needed to be taken. With the support of Lapointe and his other Quebec ministers, the prime minister acted. On August 5, 1940, the RCMP entered Montreal's City Hall and arrested the mayor. He was taken to an Ontario internment camp where he remained for the next four years. There was surprisingly little opposition to the move, even in Montreal.

By late 1942, Hitler had taken nearly all of Europe and had pushed Soviet forces so far back that Nazi soldiers could see Moscow's skyline. The seaport of Leningrad and the resource-rich area surrounding Stalingrad appeared ready to fall. Nazi submarines were becoming increasingly deadly, and U-boats were even spotted in the St. Lawrence River. Japan had entered the fray with attacks that killed Americans at Pearl Harbor and Brits and Canadians at Hong Kong. Canada had declared war on Japan.

All this bad news and the war's expansion resulted in Canada's military leaders pressing for more recruits just as C.D. Howe was bemoaning that a labour shortage was hampering his manufacturing and supply efforts. Conscription was needed, but King had promised to avoid it. In a phrase that would have brought a grin to Sir John, who never rushed a decision and always avoided being pinned down, King said he would support conscription if necessary, but not necessarily conscription.

To meet military needs while also keeping the country united through the implementation of a policy he knew could rip it apart, King approved a national plebiscite. The prime minister asked Canadians to let him off the hook with this question: "Are you in favour of releasing the Government from any obligations arising out of any past commitments restricting the methods of raising men for military service?" The campaigns on both sides were equally passionate, but the yes side was clearly going to win. When the votes were counted, 66 percent of Canadians voted yes and only 34 percent said no. Significantly, though, 73 percent of Quebecers had voted no while 80 percent of English Canada, including a majority of Ukrainian and German immigrants, had voted yes. King's authority to act on the plebiscite's result and institute conscription was made official with the passage of Bill 80 in April 1942.

Two years later, with volunteer recruitment slowing and Canada's need for more servicemen even more acute, Bill 80 was invoked. Acting on the advice of his military leaders, in November 1944, King approved the conscripting of men not just for home service, but also for fighting overseas. There was outrage expressed by many Quebecers, but the riots of the previous war were not repeated. There were no celebrations in the rest of the country, but rather a stoic acquiescence from people hardened by the sacrifices of total war. Not a single premier, not even Quebec's, spoke publicly against the measure.

By the war's end, 12,908 conscripted young Canadians had been sent to battle zones. The number is noteworthy, but relatively small when one considers that 1.1 million Canadians served. The careful manner in which the federal government approached and implemented the decision ensured that while there was opposition, especially in Quebec, the country remained united in the midst of a national emergency.

RECOVERY

It was November 1943. Canadian troops were slogging their way up the Italian boot with British and American allies while the Soviets were slowly grinding Hitler's army back from its primary cities. The beginning of the war's end was not yet nigh. There was a great debate around Canada's big, oblong cabinet table. Voices were raised. None knew how or when the war would end, but everyone knew it must end someday. None wanted a replay of the disruption, recession, and violence that followed the end of the last global war.

Like Canada, Britain concerned itself with postwar planning while the war still raged. Churchill had asked one of Britain's leading economists, Sir William Beveridge, to consider problems and opportunities. Beveridge identified want, disease, ignorance, squalor, and idleness as problems to avoid. His 1942 report suggested that a national program of responsible postwar social policy was a three-legged stool resting upon children's allowances paid to responsible parents to mitigate child poverty, medical and rehabilitation services to contribute to improved health, and a job-creating economy to afford dignity and self-reliance for people and a stable tax base for government. The federal government must, in short, play a greater role than ever before. Beveridge visited Canada, and King was among the many influential Canadians who heard him speak. King also met with him privately and was again moved by his ideas.

Despite the growing popularity and influence of Beveridge and his report, many Canadian politicians, ironically including C.D. Howe, argued that Ottawa could help best by doing less. He reminded colleagues that the federal government's money had helped to build airfields, roads, and factories, and none of that industrial capacity would vanish when the guns stopped. Furthermore, in building the war machine and making it hum, workers, managers, and industrial leaders had learned new skills that would not be forgotten. The federal government should, therefore, invest in research facilities and offer tax incentives for companies to expand. Beyond that, Ottawa should get out of the way and allow private enterprise the freedom it needed to thrive. Howe's argument was an ideological counterweight to the Beveridge perspective, but of primary significance was that it presented a debate of degrees. The federal government would remain more involved in our lives and economy than before the war.

Adding to the debate and tilting it toward more government activism, was the growing acceptance of the work of John Maynard Keynes. Keynes was the Cambridge economist and journalist who had written and spoken extensively about governments using the power of the purse to fill wallets. That is, by borrowing and spending during bad times, governments could stimulate growth and then repay the debt when good times returned. Keynes was an influential presence at the 1944 Bretton Woods Conference, where, with Canada in attendance, the global postwar economy was planned based largely on his ideas. He was also an important advocate for the creation of the International Monetary Fund (IMF). It worked to establish fixed exchange rates to bring stability to global trade and commerce.

King had advocated a laissez-faire approach in the 1920s and early 1930s, but those days were over. He was a trained economist who carefully considered the new economic and social ideas and came to place more value than he had before in active interventions such as those that had marked Sir John's tenure. Rather than surrender the future solely to the profit motive and allow the whims and wisdom of private investors to plot a path, he would have Ottawa play a more direct role in moving the country toward sustainable postwar prosperity. The government's January 1944 Speech from the Throne reflected the changing times and perspective with announcements regarding a national pension plan, children's allowances, and unemployment insurance. There would be a skills-training program for returning veterans. To oversee the transition to peacetime, King created three new departments: Veterans Affairs, National Health and Welfare, and Reconstruction.

After a good deal of wrangling, Howe was placed in charge of the new Department of Reconstruction. Through his herculean efforts, and while still all but running Canada's major resource and manufacturing industries, the federal government began the process of decoupling control while still setting direction. Among the most influential initiatives was granting companies double depreciation allowances to mitigate the costs of converting factories to peacetime pursuits. From 1944 to its phasing out two years later, over $25 million helped companies make necessary adjustments.

The Department of Reconstruction created the War Assets Corporation, which was later renamed the Crown Assets Disposal Corporation. It prepared to sell what the federal government had bought or built during the war. It would sell factories, land, buildings, tools, and equipment to companies that would spin them back into privately owned manufacturing centres. Corning Glass, for example, would come to Canada with the purchase of the federal government's Research Enterprises plant in Leaside. In nearby Malton, Britain's A.V. Roe Company would build aircraft in the government's former wartime facilities. Canada's wartime shipyards would be converted, disassembled, or sold piecemeal. Naval ships and various classes of vessels would be sold at garage-sale prices to shipping companies that would use them to move manufactured and agricultural products to the world.

In April 1945, Ottawa released its White Paper on Employment and Income. The discussion document clearly advocated moving Canada to the Beveridge-Keynes camp. It called for a commitment to a high and stable level of employment. It also supported tariff changes to increase trade, tax credits to help businesses convert to the production of consumer goods, government-run research facilities to bring innovation to agriculture and industry, and a new Industrial Development Bank to help businesses secure financing. The white paper also advocated augmenting family allowances, unemployment insurance, and pensions. The programs, it said, would help people while also making it more likely that they would buy the products businesses would be producing, thereby keeping the consumer-driven economy growing.

At the end of April, Adolf Hitler did the world a great service. With bombs demolishing Berlin and his command shrinking to not much beyond the concrete bunker in which he had taken refuge, the Führer took a revolver in hand and blew out what was left of his brains. In early August, a single American plane lumbered over the skies of Hiroshima and then another found Nagasaki. The war was over.

Due to the federal government's careful planning, Canada was ready for peace. Businesses and the jobs they created converted quickly. Washing machines were made instead of guns. Cars for suburban driveways rolled off assembly lines that had produced trucks for the battlefield. The returning veterans were absorbed into workplaces booming with products and potential.

A fascinating aspect of the federal government's planning, programs, and far-reaching legislation that allowed it to provide sterling wartime leadership is that the provinces were either shunted aside or largely ignored. They had each passed important legislation and created patriotic and helpful programs as each addressed important areas of concern. However, just as the war had demanded a national perspective, postwar prosperity was, as the 1945 white paper noted, "a great national objective." There was no room for the old power squabbles based on parsing interpretations of constitutional phrases. The war had been won and there was a nation to rebuild. It would be done in two ways and it would be tough. It would be tougher than anyone imagined.

5

CONCRETE AND COMMUNITY

The Wild West was wild indeed. When Sir John became prime minister in 1867, Canada's western frontier was the hardwood wilderness of Georgian Bay's rugged shore. Macdonald knew he led a skeletal country and that if it were to survive long enough to avoid being bombed, bought, or bamboozled into becoming American, it needed a railway to tie the Atlantic and Pacific. When engineers began planning the route, the only way to move from one end of the country to the other was by canoe. The federal government's massive and audacious infrastructure project allowed Canada to grow and thrive.

At the end of the Second World War, Canada faced a similar moment of angst and opportunity. In the dark and desperate days of the war, when it looked as if Britain might fall and Canada and the United States might be the West's last bastion, Prime Minister King and President Roosevelt had inexorably linked their countries' defence and economies. It was an obviously unequal partnership, but one that benefited both. The wartime agreement and board survived and adjusted to the outbreak of peace. They helped Canada while shaping and also threatening its sovereignty. Canadian government leaders accepted the new reality, but at the same time initiated infrastructure projects and community building programs to boost economic opportunity, maintain Canada's uniqueness, and avoid being swallowed by a benevolent friend that no longer needed to attack to conquer.

An important element in the postwar nation-building era was that, in 1949, the Louis St. Laurent government had taken the final steps in moving Canada from its judicial adolescence by ending the power of Britain's Judicial Committee of the Privy Council. Legislation stipulated that the Canadian Supreme Court would be the true court of last resort for Canadians feeling unjustly treated in lower courts or by their governments and in the interminable federal-provincial power contests. Quebec led provincial opposition to cutting old colonial ties with the argument that the JCPC was a necessary restraint on federal power. It was noted that without the Lords acting as overlords, Canada would be the world's only democratic state in which the head of government had unfettered power to appoint justices to the judicial body responsible for adjudicating over that government's actions. Provincial concerns notwithstanding, the Canadian Supreme Court was finally rendered supreme in another important step toward obtaining full sovereignty. There was more to come, and it came as concrete and community.

CONCRETE

It was Henry Ford's fault. As canals were to the 18th century and railways to the 19th, highways were to the 20th. Sir John's railway established and then strengthened Canada's east-west orientation in the face of north-south temptations. A new and bold nation-building infrastructure project, a transcontinental highway, would do it again.

The federal government had attempted to get into the road business in 1913 with the passage of Bill 32. The Senate squashed the bill on the grounds that road building and maintenance were provincial responsibilities. The provinces forged ahead alone. Ontario led the way with its creation of the Provincial Highways Department in 1917. Other provinces followed suit. Their primary goal was to bolster agricultural output by linking rural production to urban markets while helping the tourism industry by tying cities to lakes. Provinces taxed, licensed, and regulated cars and drivers.

The First World War changed minds and pushed constitutional considerations aside. Ottawa's 1919 Canada Highways Act provided money equivalent to 40 percent of costs to provinces that submitted five-year road-building plans. While urging the provinces to build a network that would eventually allow for cross-Canada travel, none looked beyond their immediate goals to the national vision. Road construction became prohibitively expensive as more traffic and bigger trucks forced more stringent highway standards. Provinces saw licensing as a cash cow, but the enormous revenues were being outstripped by burgeoning road and highway construction and maintenance costs. R.B. Bennett allocated $20 million to road construction as part of a Depression-era job-creation program. This money came with strings and one was that roads must move toward binding Canada together. For the first time, people heard the words *Trans-Canada Highway*.

During the Second World War, the completion of the 190-mile Big Bend Highway that connected Revelstoke and Golden, British Columbia, made it possible to drive from Halifax to Vancouver without detouring through the United States. The trip would have been arduous, though, as cars would bump along over great sections of substandard and unpaved roads. A 1943 Special Parliamentary Committee on Reconstruction report suggested that provinces were ready to waive constitutional restraints so that Ottawa could take the lead in highway construction.

By the war's end, Canada had just over a half million miles of roads, but only about 18,000 miles were paved. Provinces seeking to take advantage of the postwar prosperity recognized the need to build more and pave more, mostly to support the increasing number of trucks transporting all the new manu-factured goods to eager domestic consumers. Prairie govern-ments were especially keen on building highways to compete with railways and sky-high freight rates that many believed were hindering economic progress. A 1948 Department of Mines and Resources report suggested that instead of each province approaching highway construction in a piecemeal fashion, Ottawa should undertake a grand national project. It predicted that the building of a cross-Canada highway would take 12 years and cost $200 million.

At the Liberal Party national convention a few months after the report's publication, the premiers of Saskatchewan and Nova Scotia both called for the highway's creation. King's cabinet discussed the project in December, and a consensus confirmed that the highway was good for the country. However, there was also worry that other premiers, especially Quebec's Maurice Duplessis, would see any pan-Canadian program as an intrusion into provincial jurisdiction. Provincial premiers and representatives were invited to Ottawa, and as predicted, Duplessis objected to the plan and even the meeting itself. They met without him. All those present agreed on the project's value and pledged co-operation. Shortly afterward, responsibility for the highway was transferred to C.D. Howe's Department of Reconstruction.

The project was slowed with the intervention of a national election and the installation of Louis St. Laurent as the new prime minister. The Trans-Canada Highway Act was finally passed in 1949. It stipulated a system of conditional grants. The federal government would pay up to half the costs of all the highways built since 1928 and all new construction until the highway was complete. It would pay 100 percent of construction costs through national parks. In return, provinces had to agree to routes that allowed the shortest east-west distance, coordinate with neighbouring provinces' routes, and adhere to nationally mandated specifications regarding road and shoulder widths, gradients, and more.

Despite earlier support, New Brunswick and Nova Scotia joined Quebec in arguing that the project would impinge upon provincial rights and control of their territories. All three refused to participate. Newfoundland, Canada's newest province, having joined just months before, asked for more time to study the deal and then did not agree. While fighting the nation-building project, the four intractable provinces nonetheless demanded that they receive the highway money allocated to them even if they refused to sign on or adhere to the law's conditions. St. Laurent said no. Construction commenced.

All provinces eventually agreed to become involved according to the deal originally offered. There were arguments with provinces wanting to direct the road through major centres versus the shortest east-west routes, but compromises were reached. Provinces brought a retinue of issues to a 1956 meeting, but progress continued when Ottawa agreed to pay a greater percentage of costs. For some difficult stretches such as atop Lake Superior, under the St. Lawrence River, and through the Rocky Mountains, the Canadian government's share rose to 90 percent. Provinces were allowed additional flexibility in applying national standards. Progress was slow and expensive, but inexorable. Overall, the new standards improved not just the highway, but also led to positive changes on other roads.

While additional work would be done until 1970, the Trans-Canada Highway was deemed complete in 1962. The 4,860-mile, all-weather, paved road with its specific width, grades, and straightened turns reduced accidents, boosted tourism, and increased truck traffic. It helped businesses move more products and renegotiate rail rates. It helped people move from town to town and city to cottage, and the whole country to think east-west.

Prime Minister John Diefenbaker was among the dignitaries gathered at Rogers Pass on a cool September afternoon to officially open the highway. In a nod to the last spike, he took shovel in hand and patted flat the last asphalt splat. New Brunswick and Newfoundland boycotted the event. Despite the fact that the ceremony was taking place in his province, B.C. Premier W.A.C. Bennett also missed it. Like the others, he was still demanding more funds from Ottawa. In fact, on

July 30, Bennett had conducted his own official opening, but had mentioned neither Canada nor the federal government's leadership and money. He didn't even call it the Trans-Canada Highway, but instead, B.C. Highway One. It would take until 1972 for a new B.C. premier, Dave Barrett, to end the petulance and order the hammering up of the green Trans-Canada Highway signs that were found languishing in a warehouse.

Diefenbaker was proud to have participated in the Tran-Canada Highway celebration because he sincerely believed in road construction as an important element in nation building. An unabashed Canadian nationalist whose hero was Sir John, the Prairie populist promised Canadians that as Macdonald's railway had built the country to the west, he would use roads to unlock the rich potential of the north. He called the program Roads to Resources.

The Department of Northern Affairs and National Resources saw an increase in its personnel and budget. It was mandated to develop short- and long-range tactics to bring development to a part of the country that had been largely ignored, but that with Diefenbaker's 1958 election campaign had captured Canadians' imagination. Seventy-five million dollars was allocated, deals were made with provinces and the territories, co-operation with a number of private companies was established, and the construction commenced.

From 1958 to 1963, more than 4,000 miles of roads were constructed. Some northern communities benefited from the roads and the mines that were opened and others that were expanded, but the program's great potential went unfulfilled. It was daring in its vision, but stumbled over its administrative feet. Its legacy was the platform from which the next logical steps in realizing Diefenbaker's goals could be taken. It would take a new century, another Conservative prime minister, and climate change transforming the game to bring Diefenbaker's northern dream back to the fore.

While the Trans-Canada was our newest highway, the St. Lawrence River was our first. Thousands of years ago, it carried Aboriginal traders and armies. It then led French and English adventurers to the interior in their quests to seek gold and sell God. A hundred years ago, despite some canals, including one linking Lake Erie and Lake Ontario near Welland, Ontario, and another around the Lachine Rapids near Montreal, the river and lakes that extended its reach remained much as they had always been. In 1895, the first joint Canadian-American Deep Waterways Commission was formed to look at building a unified seaway system, but nothing came of it. In 1922, another bilateral commission suggested undertaking a co-operative effort to build dams, power plants, and canals that would rob the St. Lawrence of its song, but tap into its potential. American political squabbling drowned progress. So did fights between Ottawa and Quebec City regarding which level of government owned the water and its banks and who should pay for anything that changed either.

More years saw the same old arguments circled like the mighty river's eddies. Ontario Premier Howard Ferguson and Quebec Premier Louis-Alexandre Taschereau agreed on nearly nothing. But they eventually admitted to sharing a dream of a water transportation route linking Lake Superior to the Atlantic with docking facilities and power plants along the way to feed their growing cities. They pressured a wary Prime Minister King to revive the project. King worried about technical challenges, costs, and the American exploitation of such an important Canadian resource. He also worried about the ever-present jurisdictional power squabbles, so he delayed action by asking the opinion of the Supreme Court. Its vague decision coupled with incendiary accusations of self-serving intentions and double-crossing that ricocheted between Toronto, Ottawa, and Quebec City ended up shelving the project yet again.

R.B. Bennett campaigned partly on finally getting the seaway built. In a number of 1930 campaign speeches, he drew a comparison to the inestimable power of Germany's industrial heartland: "I once called the St. Lawrence basin the Ruhr-to-be of Canada. I should more properly have termed it, the Ruhr of North America."[1] Once in office, he ordered a new investigation of the seaway's viability. He was told of technical challenges and that there would be opposition from those arguing that the project would demand flooding farm-land while despoiling the river's natural beauty. The report also warned that it would cost a fortune, American involvement would affect Canada's sovereignty, and that the whole thing would bring federal-provincial fights back to centre stage. Bennett heard the objections and then ordered the project to commence.

He travelled to Washington and met with American President Herbert Hoover in January 1931. They agreed on costs, benefits, and challenges and that it needed to be done. While Canadian and American officials secretly negotiated details, Bennett ordered greater alacrity on the stalled work on the Welland Canal that would be a part of the St. Lawrence project. Opposition critics slammed the spending of so much money during the Depression, but Bennett thundered, "Did it ever occur to honourable members that there are occasions in the lives of nations as of individuals when decisions have to be made or the opportunity is gone forever?"[2] Sir John would have been proud.

With the details of an American-Canadian co-operative venture becoming clearer, Bennett brought Ontario Premier George Henry to Ottawa. Once convinced of the advantages to his province, Henry agreed to the estimated financial contribution Ontario would make. Bennett then consulted Taschereau. Quebec's prickly premier complained about his province's share of costs, of Ottawa's intrusion into its jurisdiction, and about Bennett having spoken to Henry before him. However, Taschereau diplomatically expressed his concerns not in public but in private letters to the prime minister.

Bennett and Hoover signed the St. Lawrence Deep Waterway Treaty in July 1932. Because it was a treaty, it needed the American Senate's approval, and there it hit a series of snags. Hoover was a lame duck and an unpopular president with little residual political capital to manoeuvre it through northeastern senators worried about business potentially lost to a northern route and Midwest senators concerned about increased freight rates. Plus, the president-elect was Franklin Roosevelt. As New York's governor, FDR had argued vehemently against the seaway. The Senate refused to ratify. The seaway died.

By the early 1950s, Ontario's booming industries hugging the Great Lakes demanded more shipping and more hydroelectricity. The province needed the seaway more than ever before. After American interests created the Iron Ore Company of

Canada in 1949, it pressured Quebec Premier Duplessis to support the seaway. The company argued that with raw ore now being pulled from the ground as never before, a seaway to ship it all while boosting hydro capacity would create jobs and increase government revenue. The Quebec government soon expressed the same eagerness as Ontario to move the project forward. It was up to the federal government to make it happen.

Prime Minister St. Laurent's minister of transport, Lionel Chevrier, made a startling announcement in the House of Commons in December 1951. If the Americans were not interested in participating in the building of the St. Lawrence Seaway, then the Canadian government would do it alone. St. Laurent was not bluffing. His government created the St. Lawrence Seaway Authority, and it began planning for the big build.

With the election of Dwight Eisenhower to the presidency, St. Laurent recognized an ally in the White House. Plus, up-and-coming Senator John F. Kennedy travelled to Montreal to explain that, while his home state of Massachusetts had always opposed the seaway, he would support it as an economic boon to Canada and America's Atlantic states and a testament to Canadian-American friendship. He reminded skeptical senators that the seaway was also backed by the American defence community. In May 1954, the U.S. Senate finally voted to approve the joint project. A few months later, after intense negotiations regarding cost-sharing and ownership, the Canadian-American agreement was signed.

The seaway's construction drew international attention. Comparisons were made to the building of the Panama and Suez Canals. While the federal government and its Crown corporation took the lead in the project, the Quebec and Ontario governments played important roles. Ontario Hydro, for example, directed the relocation of 225 farms, 1,000 cottages, 10 villages and hamlets, and the rerouting of rail lines between Morrisburg and Cornwall to allow the necessary flooding along Lake Ontario's northeast shore.

Already having officiated at the opening of one manifestation of the federal government's nation building with the opening of the Trans-Canada Highway, Prime Minister Diefenbaker got to do it again in 1959. Along with Queen Elizabeth II and President Eisenhower, he proudly pointed to the St. Lawrence Seaway as having been built on time and under budget. From Lake Superior to the Atlantic, the seaway was 2,342 miles long and opened Canada's interior to deep-draft ocean-going vessels. Hydroelectric production soared, shipping boomed, cities grew, and the economic multiplier effects rippled. The country that many historians consider having been built upon the concept of the Empire of the St. Lawrence took a giant leap forward. But there was another leap to be made.

COMMUNITY

The 1960s are too often seen through a nostalgic lens. At least from 1963, the decade was indeed a sparkling renaissance of new and exciting music, theatre, fashion, art, movies, and architecture boldly going where none had gone before. It was also a time of fundamental social change. There is always as much chagrin as celebration when old rules no longer apply and frustration with advancements unevenly enjoyed. For progressive governments and transitional leaders, though, the black dots of problems offer bright lights of opportunity. Such was Canada in the 1960s.

The black and bright was evident in a number of areas and clearly in the misfortune of too many elderly Canadians. In the early 1960s, despite Canada's enjoying the longest period of economic growth and sustained prosperity in its history, a great many old people were crushingly poor. While 25 percent of Canadians found themselves beneath the poverty line, 44 percent of seniors languished there. A heartbreaking 73 percent of single or widowed women over the age of 65 suffered in poverty.

As far back as 1908, Ottawa had urged Canadians to save and plan with its Government Annuities Act. Much like the Registered Retirement Savings Plan that would arrive much later, the legislation offered people an opportunity to immediately save on taxes by squirrelling money away for their personal winter.

A growing number of impoverished seniors in the 1920s that roared for so many others proved that more needed to be done. However, the Constitution afforded provinces the power to determine social policies. Prime Minister King negotiated with premiers to establish the Old Age Security Act. It was administered by the provinces but subsidized by Ottawa. Enhancements were made in the 1930s and 1940s.

In 1951, the federal government sought to more substantively improve pensions for seniors, but a number of provinces balked. With prosperity urging compassion, bulging budgets, and promises of more money from Ottawa, however, a constitutional amendment was adopted to allow national action. Old Age Security (OAS) was instituted through which seniors in need received direct benefits. Unlike the pension plan, the OAS allowed all seniors over the age of 70, regardless of income, to collect a monthly stipend. The federal government funded half the costs and provinces paid the rest while handling administration. Individual payments were relatively small, but to those suffering the indignity of poverty after a lifetime of work, the cheques were like candles in the darkness.

In 1963, Lester Pearson's government found itself in the same situation as King in the late 1920s: there was a growing consensus that more needed to be done while a powerful left-wing party was pushing a progressive agenda on a minority Liberal government. Pearson had pledged in the 1962 and 1963 elections to create a new and better national pension plan based on the pay-as-you-go notion that we would contribute a little throughout our working lives to help others and then, in the future, working people would pay a little bit each payday to support our retirement. Like similar social programs, it reflected the broadening of the circle of community. In July 1963, Pearson's cabinet approved a plan that allowed for small contributions to be collected from workers and employers and then, after a 10-year transition period, a monthly pension would be dispensed to all Canadians over the age of 70. The plan was technically and economically sound, but a political bombshell.

Critics pounded the plan. Private insurance companies and banks led the way with claims that a national program of forced savings would hurt Canadians' ability to save on their own, presumably, but never stated, with them. The Chamber of Commerce said jobs would be lost due to forcing employers to contribute to the plan. Those on the political right spoke of the expansion of the "nanny state" that would rob us of the important value of self-reliance while creating a larger and more expensive government that was already taking too much of our money.

Provincial opposition to the pension plan rocked the spring 1964 first ministers' conference. The most vocal premier was Quebec's Jean Lesage. Elected in 1960, Lesage had been leading his province in a scramble to catch up to a modern world after what many believed, correctly or not, had been decades lost as an anachronistic, agrarian society kneeling at the cloak of the Catholic Church. The new energy and ideas were dubbed the Quiet Revolution. When presented with the pension plan, Lesage turned his new revolution toward an old idea and portrayed the plan as yet another unwelcome and unwarranted intrusion of the English-dominated federal government. The pension idea allowed Lesage to again call for Quebec to shun Ottawa to become the master of its own house.

Lesage ordered the development of an all-Quebec pension scheme. The Quebec plan would earn revenue from mandatory payroll deductions that would be paid in retirement benefits. Surplus revenue would create a pool of capital the Quebec government could use to finance Quiet Revolution economic and infrastructure development. Lesage promised to fight any Canadian scheme to interfere with his two-pronged plan.

Ontario Premier John Robarts led the other premiers in expressing support for the national pension plan's goals but asked that it be delayed. He explained that insurance companies and a number of other companies were already providing pensions for great numbers of Ontarians. Furthermore, Robarts said that because the Constitution placed pensions in the provincial sphere, he would simply opt out should Ottawa pass national pension legislation. Pearson's plan appeared dead.

But then Ottawa made a deal with Quebec. The province could create and administer its own pension plan. At one point Premier Robarts floated the idea of beginning an Ontario plan similar to Quebec's, but after intense negotiations he signed on to the national program. The other provinces were also consulted and agreed.

The pension negotiations involved a constitutional amendment to allow the new pan-Canadian plan and for it to also include widows' benefits. The amendment was an important step that should be seen in context with two others. In 1940, unemployment insurance had been added to the federal government's Section 91 powers. A 1951 amendment stated that old-age pensions were a concurrent or shared responsibility between the two levels of government. These amendments and Pearson's creation of the Canadian Pension Plan (CPP) were significant steps away from the vision of Canada for which provinces had previously fought and which the Judicial Committee of the Privy Council had enabled. They were what the 1940 Rowell-Sirois Commission had encouraged. The amendments and social legislation they allowed signified that Canada was moving forward by moving back toward Sir John's original vision of a federal government having sufficient power to play a leadership role in using the state to build the nation.

The bill creating the CPP was brought to the House in 1965 and came into effect a year later. It had employers and employees paying 3.6 percent of salaries with exemptions for low-income earners. Ottawa would establish a trust fund to ensure stability during the transition period, after which the plan would be self-sustaining. The qualifying age would then be lowered from 70 to 65 years of age. Quebec would keep its unique pension plan. All other provinces would administer the national plan, but in the future they could opt out as Quebec had and create their own as long as they, too, met national standards. The provinces would also enjoy the power to veto any future changes to the Canadian plan. The legislation also stated that half of the pension reserve fund collected by the federal government would be transferred back to the provinces. Surplus money could be spent on roads or schools or other projects of their choosing just as Quebec would be spending its surplus pension revenue. Federal Health and Welfare Minister Judy LaMarsh explained that, with the provinces' concurrence, the federal government had created a national plan that allowed all Canadians to enjoy retirement security that for generations had been but a dream for so many.

With the understanding that the CPP would be phased in but that seniors needed immediate help, Ottawa increased the OAS by $10 a month and created a new program called the Guaranteed Income Supplement (GIS). It was designed as a monthly top-up for seniors who needed help. While originally seen as temporary, it remained in place after the CPP's transition period ended. While there was the predictable opposition from predictable quarters, no province offered resistance to the GIS's creation or complained when it continued beyond its best-before date.

With provincial support, the federal government later introduced changes that indexed CPP benefits to inflation and ensured survival benefits for spouses and split benefits after a divorce. Canadians would later be allowed to begin collecting a reduced pension at age 60 along with same-sex and common-law spouse benefits. With the vagaries of economic ups and downs and the anticipated pressures from the baby boom generation's retirement, the Canadian government created the Canada Pension Plan Board to invest CPP income. Its long-term viability was guaranteed. Opposition to the CPP faded as it became interwoven into the fabric of what it meant to be a Canadian. The federal government had fulfilled one of its roles and had extended community's circle.

Pearson's government went on to create two more important elements in the foundation of Canada's national community. The Canada Assistance Plan (CAP) built upon already existing support for unemployed Canadians. Through negotiation with the provinces, the CAP established new and less stringent criteria for people to qualify for help. It also supported programs to alleviate the root causes of their needing help in the first place. Employment training, child-care support, and drug and alcohol addiction programs, for instance, were instituted. As with the Canada Pension Plan, the federal government paid 50 percent of the CAP's costs and set national standards while administration fell to the provinces. Also like the CPP, there were ongoing negotiations and deals regarding special provincial or regional circumstances that led to program tweaks.

Then there was Medicare. The concept of community, the basis of all national social policies, is tested at the bedside of a sick child. Should I pay a little so that the child's worried parent, a person I will never meet, can afford to obtain the necessary medical help to make her well? Due to our shared citizenship, is that child my child? Is it the federal government's job to encourage answers to such questions and then provide a vehicle to act upon the moral imperative?

The questions were first asked in Saskatchewan. In 1947 Premier Tommy Douglas enacted North America's first government-controlled, universal, single-pay medical insurance plan. Insurance companies fought it. Chambers of Commerce fought it. Doctors fought it. In fact, when the legislation passed, 90 percent of Saskatchewan's doctors went on strike for nearly a month. Douglas stood his ground.

Saskatchewan native Prime Minister John Diefenbaker established a Royal Commission to examine the possibility of creating a national health-care plan based on Douglas's daring initiative. Insurance companies and doctors attacked again. But the Hall Commission's report suggested that a national health-care plan was essential for the country. It suggested that we should pay for things from which we derive benefit and that we all benefit from living in a society with healthy people and where catastrophic illness does not spell bankruptcy. Pearson's government acted on the report and found premiers receptive to yet another deal whereby Ottawa would offer 50 percent of funding and the establishment of national standards for a program administered by them. The National Medical Care Insurance Act stated that medical coverage would be a truly national program, since it would be based on Canadian citizenship and not provincial residency. Benefits would be universal. The bill creating the national health-care program passed the House of Commons in December 1966 with a vote of 177 to 2.

Canada's health-care system has never been perfect. Nothing is ever perfect. But it represented an important concept. Prime Minister Pearson had explained it well at a November 1963 first ministers' conference. In words that could have been spoken by Sir John, he said that Ottawa would take the lead in advancing national interests. It would do so in a new era of co-operation based on "a mutual respect for the jurisdictions and the responsibilities of Canada and the Provinces … timely and reliable two-way consultation as the basis for co-ordinating the parallel action … sharing is not only equitable between the federal government and the Provinces generally, but also is equitable among the Provinces themselves …"[3] These principles were essential to the development of the social welfare state that had been slowly growing since the 1920s and was continuing to coalesce in the sustained postwar prosperity.

The principles did not mean, however, that provincial fights for money and power would end — far from it. In fact, the notion of co-operative federalism, or its cousin, fiscal federalism, invited even more dissent. The debates became especially heated when costs for various programs increased or the federal government tinkered with its funding formulas or national standards. However, the new era of co-operative federalism that was expressed in programs involving concrete and community were based on the reality that if left to their own political impulses and fiscal capabilities, most provinces were unable to meet their responsibilities, or even if so inclined, to do much to enrich the concept of national citizenship. Only the federal government's leadership and capacities are up to that essential task.

The social legislation Pearson saw passed, when considered in concert with the pan-Canadian infrastructure initiatives, essentially said that Canadians had grown tired of provincial and regional politics that tried to ignore, belittle, or shunt aside common purpose. We wanted Ottawa and the provinces to work together and consider us not pawns, but citizens with all such a noble concept demanded and celebrated. The 1960s moment was as stirring as the patriotic bubble of Expo 67 and the many centennial projects that marked Canada's 100th birthday. But all parties end. All bubbles burst. The decade that boasted such promise and progress ended with the Beatles splitting up, and then we nearly did, too.

6

RIGHTS AND RESOURCES

When a waterhole begins to dry up, the animals look at one another a little differently. In the early 1970s, the long period of post–Second World War prosperity sputtered. There were a number of contributory factors. New communications and transportation advances and economic growth in places that had not seen it before led to a shift of industrial and manufacturing jobs out of the country. Increased rates of urbanization and immigration affected cities. Declining commodity prices hurt a number of economic sectors, and then the entry of millions of baby boomers into the workforce boosted consumer prices, pressured housing, and stressed job markets. Deficits and debts grew as the federal and provincial governments borrowed to meet fiscal obligations in a sea of overlapping and nearly overwhelming changes. Options sank as their inability to impose domestic tranquility in the face of global hurricanes sank in. And the federal and provincial governments started to look at each other differently.

Except for a nine-month interruption, throughout the 1968 to 1984 period of challenge and change, a former journalist and constitutional law professor named Pierre Elliott Trudeau led the federal government. One moment offers the man's defining metaphor. Trudeau was one of three respected Quebecers Pearson invited to contest the 1965 election. Trudeau accepted primarily to fight those trying to exploit Quebec's Quiet Revolution with angry ethnic nationalism and an intention to create a separate Quebec state. One separatist faction sought to accomplish the goal through democratic evolution and the other through violent revolution. The revolutionaries robbed banks and bombed symbols of the Canadian government such as post office boxes. They appeared unmoved by the innocent people they hurt and killed.

After serving as parliamentary secretary and justice minister, and with Pearson's retirement, Trudeau won the Liberal leadership. The late spring and summer campaign of 1968 saw the odd spectacle of what was dubbed Trudeaumania. Trudeau was undeniably charismatic and a natural performance artist who seemed to answer the longing for our own John F. Kennedy. On the day before we were to go to the polls, Trudeau was among the dignitaries gathered on an elevated gallery enjoying Montreal's Saint-Jean-Baptiste Day parade. Angered by the Canadian government's representative having such a prominent spot at Quebec's annual celebration, revolutionary separatists began shouting and swearing at Trudeau. They chanted, "Trudeau to the gallows!" When bottles and rocks began raining down, the dignitaries scattered and Trudeau's security detail tried to haul him from danger. The prime minister shook them off. He waved for the others to run if they wished, resumed his seat, hung his arms defiantly over the bunting before him, and scowled defiantly at the protesters. Trudeau stood his ground.

The ground upon which he stood was Sir John's. Like Macdonald, Trudeau saw Canada not as a collection of provinces or, as his Conservative rival Joe Clark would argue, a community of communities. Rather, he and Sir John saw Canada as a unified whole and the prime minister's job to fight against the centrifugal forces of provincialism and regionalism that weaken it. Throughout Trudeau's administrations, many provinces contributed to those forces, but of special significance were Quebec and Alberta. The first battlefield of the 1970s and 1980s power wars resembled an actual field of battle. As usual, the federal government was called upon to save the day.

On October 5, 1970, a cell of the loosely organized Front de libération du Québec (FLQ) kidnapped British Trade Commissioner James Cross from his Montreal home. He was seen as a symbol of British imperialism stifling Quebec's aspirations. A number of ransom demands were made, including the release of FLQ members in jail for bank robberies and violent acts but who their comrades called "political prisoners." Quebec's Deputy Premier and Labour Minister Pierre Laporte refused all ransom demands. Five days later, Laporte was kidnapped.

No one knew who might be kidnapped next or possibly marked for assassination. Trudeau ordered the Canadian military to guard public officials and other possible targets at their offices and homes. The action, he said, would allow the RCMP and overstressed Quebec police to be relieved from such duties to better focus on apprehending the kidnappers. A reporter stopped Trudeau on the Parliament Buildings' front steps and demanded a justification for the use of armed troops. Trudeau engaged in a spontaneous Socratic debate and stated, "Yes, well, there are a lot of bleeding hearts around who just don't like to see people with helmets and guns. All I can say is, go on and bleed, but it is more important to keep law and order in the society than to be worried about weak-kneed people who don't like the looks —"[1]

The country split. A surprising number of Quebecers sympathized with the kidnappers, including many union leaders and Université du Québec students who signed the FLQ manifesto. Quebec Premier Robert Bourassa wavered. From his secure suite in the Queen Elizabeth Hotel, he argued one day for stronger measures and more of Ottawa's help and another for negotiations with the terrorists. Montreal Mayor Jean Drapeau demanded federal government action in the face of "apprehended insurrection." The phrase was not a mistake. It was taken from the Canadian legislation that justified the implementation of the War Measures Act. Drapeau and Bourassa both formally asked Trudeau to bring the full measure of the federal government's power to bear.

Trudeau invoked the War Measures Act. Tanks rumbled down Montreal streets. Arrests were made. Searches were undertaken. And in Montreal, Pierre Laporte was strangled by his captors with the chain that held his silver crucifix. His body was left in a car trunk at the St. Hubert airport. The murder shocked the country.

The House of Commons overwhelmingly supported the

War Measures Act's imposition. NDP leader Tommy Douglas was among the few who did not. He argued that Trudeau was using a sledgehammer to crack a peanut. Trudeau replied, "This criticism doesn't take the facts into account. First, peanuts don't make bombs, don't take hostages, and don't assassinate prisoners. And as for the sledgehammer, it was the only tool at our disposal."[2]

There were no more bombings. There were no more kidnappings. The Laporte murder quieted those who supported revolution in theory but were repulsed by its grim reality. After two months of captivity, James Cross was released in exchange for his kidnappers being flown to Cuba.

Many at the time and later debated the use of the War Measures Act and some decried what they called a stunning example of federal government overreach. Certainly, many RCMP actions were appalling as people who obviously had no ties to the kidnappers or the FLQ were jailed. However, a poll taken just after its imposition revealed that 87 percent of Canadians, including a majority of Quebecers, supported it. Ottawa had responded to a crisis with the calm, power, and authority that Quebec's government could not muster. Trudeau's government had stood up to the terrorists as he had personally stood up to the Saint-Jean-Baptiste Day thugs two years earlier.

The most important legacy of the FLQ Crisis was that after the federal government's decisive action, the two-pronged Quebec separatist movement was reduced to one. The revolutionary element withered. From that point forward, Quebec's future, and with it Canada's fate, would be decided through peaceful, democratic means.

THE CONSTITUTION

More than a century after Sir John and his colleagues had written the Canadian Constitution it remained in name and in fact the British North America Act. That is, it was still a British law. Canada had become independent of Britain and sovereign in every way imaginable and yet, in order to change our Constitution, we still had to apply, hat in hand, to the British government and ask if it might please amend its law to please us.

The federal government made several attempts to end this increasingly embarrassing vestige of colonialism. Provincial premiers stymied each one. The sad retinue of resistance began in November 1927 when Prime Minister King convened a first ministers' conference to address a number of social and economic issues and the nagging constitutional question. Ernest Lapointe, his minister of justice and Quebec lieutenant, was in the chair. Lapointe proposed that the Constitution be secured under Canadian control. He reported that Britain was eager to comply. He said the federal government was willing to agree that once the Constitution was in Ottawa, any "ordinary changes" would require the support of the majority of the provinces. "Fundamental changes," such as those affecting provincial powers or minority rights, would need the consent of all provinces. It sounded reasonable. The provinces thought otherwise. Ontario and Quebec tackled the idea first. The others piled on. Canada's Constitution remained a Westminster law.

The provinces' determined insistence on trusting London more than Ottawa affected the imperial conference held two years later. British government representatives said that, due to the failure of 1927, legislation it had prepared to grant Canada full legal autonomy would be shelved. The issue came back to the vision of Canada that provinces had been promoting for generations to the chagrin of Canadian leaders and in defiance of Sir John's wishes. Over the next 30 years, the Constitution was amended nine times and each required an appeal to London. The federal government continued to attempt to bring Canada out of its legal childhood, but failed each time. The early 1960s brought greater urgency to the question of constitutional adulthood when Ottawa's attempts at nation building met the nation-building project of Quebec.

Like the 1860s, the 1960s saw the world flush with attempts to create states to reflect and protect nations. Nowhere was it more evident than in Africa and Southeast Asia. Borders that had been established by colonial powers and had ignored ethnic divisions were being redrawn in blood. Many nationalist fights to end colonial power became civil wars complicated by the Cold War. Atrocities were visited on the innocent. Quebec's Quiet Revolution was born in this milieu. The bombs exploding on Montreal streets echoed those dropping from African and Vietnamese skies.

The yearnings for a new Quebec state to defend and enrich the old *pure laine* nation were piled atop the provincial compact theory of Confederation. Quebec's Lesage government was not wild with revolutionaries, but it was happy to link the two ideas to increase its province's power and become a master of its own house. Other provinces appeared happy to ride the tiger.

With these ever-dangerous centrifugal forces gaining potency, Prime Minister Diefenbaker tried to fashion a consensus over an amending formula that would allow Canada's Constitution to come home. At yet another first ministers' conference, his justice minister, E. Davie Fulton, proposed that amendments affecting all provinces would need unanimous consent, but those affecting only one or more would need the consent of just those provinces. Changes that did not affect provincial powers would need the consent of two-thirds of the provinces representing over 50 percent of the country's population. It seemed reasonable. All but Saskatchewan agreed.

Four years later, Pearson's justice minister, Guy Favreau, proposed the same idea, and this time all agreed. However, after leaving the conference, conferring with his cabinet, and feeling the wrath of the province's growing sovereignist element, Quebec Premier Lesage withdrew his support.

As Pearson's justice minister, Pierre Trudeau called constitutional negotiations a "can of worms" to be avoided. However, as prime minister, three factors changed his mind. The first was the gathering vigour of French-Canadian nationalism. The second was his government's challenges in implementing the many social programs Pearson's government had initiated. Finally, there was the Confederation of Tomorrow Conference that had been organized as part of 1967's celebration of Canada's 100th birthday.

The brainchild of Ontario Premier John Robarts, the November Confederation of Tomorrow Conference brought premiers from eight provinces and representatives from the other two to Toronto. Prime Minister Pearson was invited, but, as John A. Macdonald had, declined to attend a meeting where the Canadian government would be treated as simply one at the table and not the spokesperson for the entire country. The conference's ostensible goal was to discuss Canada's future on a number of fronts, but it quickly degenerated into provinces listing complaints and squabbles among themselves. The toughest moment saw Quebec Premier Daniel Johnson demanding more and unique powers. Newfoundland Premier Joey Smallwood wagged his finger, and in a voice rising in volume and bile, insisted that the Constitution should not be changed simply to accommodate Quebec nor should French be forced on all Canadians. Observers were left to wonder how Ottawa could bring the provinces to agreement with its vision if they were split among themselves? But then, how could a responsible federal government allow such divergent visions of Canada to fester and so threaten the country? The most positive outcome of the provincial initiative was the shared recognition that constitutional work needed to be done and that Canada's government must take a lead role. Pearson continued to work diligently and justice minister and soon-to-be prime minister Trudeau came to agree that the constitutional "can of worms" had to be opened for the necessary fundamental changes to be made.

In the spring of 1971, Trudeau dispatched senior aides and cabinet ministers to determine exactly what the premiers wanted. Then he organized a June first ministers' conference in Victoria. Provinces asked for more money for social programs but less direction and interference from Ottawa in how it was spent. Trudeau insisted on national standards for those programs to avoid Canada's balkanization and the creation of different classes of Canadians. Trudeau also proposed a charter of rights. It was slighter than what would come later but necessary, he said, to protect Canadians as citizens of the whole country and not just residents of a particular province.

Premiers were cool to the notion of a charter but agreed. They insisted on a constitutional amendment to create provincial paramountcy over labour training, unemployment insurance, and family allowances. Where there was a conflict between provincial and Canadian laws, the provincial law would prevail. They also demanded an end to the federal government's ability to disallow and to reserve provincial laws. They agreed on a formula to amend the Constitution and even accepted Quebec Premier Robert Bourassa's insistence on a Quebec veto over future amendments and a guarantee that three of the nine Supreme Court justices would always be Quebecers.

Late nights and hard bargaining finally brought unanimous agreement. All were happy. But not for long. Bourassa returned to Quebec and was slammed by critics who said he had surrendered too much provincial autonomy, especially given that a charter of rights would cede so much power to the Supreme Court. They also said he had failed to secure sufficient provincial autonomy with respect to social programs. Bourassa phoned Trudeau and rescinded his agreement. He would not sign what had been dubbed the Victoria Charter.

Trudeau had been angered during the pre-negotiations and at the conference by the premiers' unwillingness to consider a national perspective. Bourassa's betrayal left him flabbergasted. He was infuriated not just with the double cross, but also with provincial demands that would have left the federal government emasculated and Canadians without a national voice. Trudeau later wrote of his refusal to surrender to Quebec's demands with the prescient warning of insatiable provincial appetites: "If we had agreed, I saw this as the beginning of a trend in which, eventually, other provinces would want to do the same thing and the government of Canada would end up being the tax collector for a confederation of shopping centres."[3] He told aides that he would put the constitutional worms back in the can for a long, long time. He tried. He failed.

René Lévesque was a charismatic, chain-smoking, fast-talking former journalist who had been an influential Lesage cabinet minister. A staunch supporter of provincial rights and a passionate Quebec sovereignist, he left the provincial Liberals and in 1968 formed the Parti Québécois (PQ). Within eight years, he led the party to victory and became Quebec's premier.

Lévesque's government enacted a number of policies that flew in the face of a broad national consensus. Included among them was a more stringent law enforcing the fact that, while Canada was officially bilingual, Quebec would have only one language. In 1980, Lévesque announced that a referendum would ask Quebecers if they supported his government negotiating a deal with the federal government whereby the province would be economically linked to Canada but politically separate. He called it sovereignty-association. Once the deal was inked, he said, a second referendum would ask for their support to implement it. Quebecers would have to vote no to say yes to Canada.

Lévesque's campaign began masterfully. His caucus delivered a carefully planned and persuasive analysis of the advantages of sovereignty-association. Members then fanned the province presenting calm and lucid arguments while equating Quebec's independence to African nations chucking chains of colonialism. National politicians and the Anglo elite were called White Rhodesians. Canada was belittled as a concept and Canadians dismissed as naive while the advantages of Confederation espoused by esteemed heroes such as Cartier, Laurier, and Lapointe were dismissed or ignored. Polls indicated that Lévesque's sovereignty-association, the yes side, would win.

Quebec Liberal leader Claude Ryan led the no side. But his popularity was as low as his charisma and persuasive ability. His campaign lacked organization and passion. Ryan was stubborn and refused Ottawa's help but seemed unable to help himself. Trudeau's Liberals had lost the 1979 election to Joe Clark's Progressive Conservative Party. Trudeau had pledged to resign as the Liberal Party leadership. Nine months later, however, Clark's minority government fell. Trudeau was persuaded to shave his retirement beard and return. In a winter election, Canadians returned him to office with a stunning majority. He took office on April 15, 1980, the same day that Lévesque announced his referendum. Disappointed by Ryan's muddled referendum campaign, Trudeau recognized that the federal government needed to act to save Canada. As polls continued to show Ryan's side sliding, Trudeau told him flatly that he was all but taking over the no campaign.

Jean Chrétien, Trudeau's justice minister, effectively reorganized and led the no side just as Lévesque's people made a number of unforced errors. Trudeau was held in reserve with the belief that four carefully timed speeches would be more powerful than several. On May 14, just six days before the vote, Trudeau appeared at a boisterous no-side rally at Montreal's Paul Sauvé Arena.

Trudeau tore Lévesque's logic to shreds. He said that the referendum was asking Quebecers to support the negotiation of sovereignty-association with the federal government but that he would not negotiate. No prime minister would negotiate Canada's demise. There would be no Quebec sovereignty, so there would be no association. On the other hand, he would welcome Lévesque and other premiers to discuss renewed federalism within a united Canada. But, Trudeau observed, Lévesque had already said he was not interested in such a discussion. Therefore, those considering voting yes must understand that they would really be saying yes to the status quo. Those wanting positive change must vote no to the trick question. Trudeau then turned to emotion. He responded to Lévesque's having questioned the legitimacy of his Quebec roots by insulting his middle name: Elliott. Trudeau blasted Lévesque for stooping to such divisive tactics and for the effects the entire campaign was having on Quebec families and the whole country. To thundering applause, Trudeau said he was a proud Quebecer as well as a proud Canadian.

Even Trudeau's critics praised the speech. It spoke to the head and heart. It married passion and reason. It clearly established the federal government's voice as Canada's voice in the provincial debate. The polls swung. Over 85 percent of eligible voters cast a ballot and 59.56 percent said no. They voted to stay in Canada. Lévesque appeared before his supporters on the same stage from which Trudeau had spoken only days before. He wept. Many before him wiped away tears. He said the fight was not over, since he was interpreting the result as Quebecers saying, "Wait until next time." He promised to hold Trudeau to his word and negotiate a renewed federalism, while fighting for Quebec.

Trudeau rushed to fulfill his promise by capturing the moment. Surely, with the country just having come to the brink of destruction, the premiers would be willing to see beyond their parochial concerns, consider themselves Canadian, and agree to changes to strengthen Canada, including the patriation of the Constitution. It was a nice thought, but Trudeau knew it would not be easy. With a majority of Quebecers having voiced their support for a nationalist vision,

Trudeau was still dealing with a minority of Albertans acting more like separatists than the separatists.

OIL

It started a half billion years ago. Hydrocarbons were formed in sedimentary rocks beneath the surface of what would become portions of Canada. Aboriginal peoples used the black gunk gurgling on the surface to seal their boats. In the 1850s, unsightly wooden oil-drilling equipment began drawing crude oil from sites in Southwestern Ontario, but the stuff was contaminated with sulphur. Then, in 1947, a discovery of oil near Leduc, Alberta, soon revealed that there was an underground sea of the purer stuff ready to be pulled up and pumped out into the burgeoning postwar economy with all its big, chrome-laden cars and swelling suburbs. When added to the natural gas that had been discovered near Medicine Hat in the 1880s, Alberta began its move from an economy centred less on growing stuff on the land to pulling stuff from beneath it. Calgary-based American multinational corporations started meeting the seemingly insatiable demand for oil and gas.

Peter Lougheed became Alberta's premier in 1971. He understood that, like all good things, the oil would not last forever. He sought to exploit the wealth and power it temporarily afforded to build a nest egg called the Heritage Fund while using the windfall to create greater economic diversity. The multinationals screamed but paid up when he raised their royalty rates. When the Oil Producing and Exporting Countries (OPEC) cut production and precipitously increased world prices in 1973, Canadians decried the skyrocketing price of gas for our cars and oil for our furnaces. American shortages that led to long gas station lines did not happen in Canada, but there were questions about supply as the price of oil kept going higher and higher and with no end in sight.

A deal had been struck in the early 1960s whereby oil west of the Ontario-Quebec boundary was supplied by domestic sources, almost all from Alberta, and east of the line from foreign sources, mostly Venezuela. The division worked well until OPEC's action resulted in a widening gulf between the prices of the two sources of oil and, therefore, the prices Canadians paid in different parts of the country. Trudeau began looking for solutions to the complex price-and-supply problems and for its devastating effects on the Canadian economy. Oil was spurring inflation and raising the price of nearly everything. The vast and growing wealth of Alberta and the relative shrinking of other provincial and regional economies were testing the ability of the federal government to maintain equalization payments that had been established to mitigate regional differences. Trudeau looked west. Lougheed glared back.

Trudeau announced a series of measures to stabilize and unify the price Canadians paid for oil and gas, ensure greater security of access, encourage more Canadian ownership of oil production, and earn more revenue. Domestic oil prices would be temporarily frozen. Ottawa would create a Crown corporation, Petro-Canada, as a wedge into the industry. New export taxes would reduce the amount of Canadian oil going to the United States. American multinationals would no longer be allowed to deduct provincial royalty payments from their federal taxes. A pipeline from Windsor, Ontario, to Montreal would be constructed, and the old line demarcating two sources and prices of oil would be erased.

Lougheed exploded. He said that Trudeau was helping Canadians by hurting Albertans and violating the Constitution. Sir John had listed natural resources as a provincial responsibility back when no one could have guessed that oil and gas would become so important to Canadian lives and businesses or that the revenues could be so massive. Lougheed portrayed Trudeau's action as an example of the federal government's long-standing habit of treating the West as a colony and doing only what benefited central Canadian business and financial interests.

Compromises were made and Canadian prices slowly rose to world prices, but the harsh feelings remained toxic when, in 1979, the Iranian Revolution led to another dramatic round of global oil-price hikes. In 1973, a barrel of oil was $2.59. In November 1979, it was $25. It then rose to $34, with experts predicting an inconceivable $100 a barrel. The Alberta government and U.S. multinationals again reaped enormous revenues while the vast majority of Canadians watched their pockets get picked. They also saw robed OPEC oil ministers on TV meeting to cut production and raise prices again, and some began calling Lougheed a blue-eyed sheik.

Trudeau's October 1980 budget presented a solution to the oil-based economic crisis. The National Energy Program (NEP) had four goals that were similar to Trudeau's previous actions. It was designed to mitigate reliance on foreign supply, increase Canadian ownership, regulate the industry to stabilize prices for consumers while allowing businesses more predictable cost projections, and increase the federal government's revenue to fund domestic oil exploration.

Premier Lougheed characterized the NEP as an attack on Alberta by eastern socialists and an out-of-control federal government concerned only with central Canadian needs. He announced a cut of 180,000 barrels a day. He refused to grant new exploration licences and promised a constitutional fight. Trudeau's energy minister, Marc Lalonde, told a reporter that the federal government had just fought a referendum in which the Quebec government demanded economic association and political sovereignty. It would not now surrender to Alberta's demands for political association but economic sovereignty.

The comparison was not well received in Calgary. Some Albertans began speaking of a Quebec-like separation. Bumper stickers appeared on Alberta vehicles: LET THOSE EASTERN BASTARDS FREEZE IN THE DARK.

It was time, Trudeau suggested, for Albertans to think more like Canadians and sacrifice a little for the good of all. Trudeau nonetheless later wrote of respecting Lougheed: "It wasn't his job as premier to take the broad view of what is good for Canada. Every provincial premier must fight for his own province. It is nice to hope that premiers would be thinking of Canada and the provinces at the same time, but it is their job to think of the provinces first — and it was my job to think of the whole country first."[4] Meanwhile, more of the anti-eastern bumper stickers appeared on more Alberta vehicles.

The fight lasted nearly a year. The federal government's debt and deficit rose as oil was subsidized to help people and businesses weather the storm caused by world prices going up and Alberta production staying down. After many tough meetings, Alberta was ceded the power to regulate the Petroleum Incentive Grants whereby federal money would support Canadian companies undertaking new oil exploration. The national export tax on natural gas was removed. A schedule was established whereby domestic oil prices would eventually meet world prices. Lougheed and Trudeau signed the agreement deemed good for both Alberta and Canada and, in a ceremony the premier later regretted, they toasted each other with expensive champagne.

Another of Canada's rich resources is its artistic talent. In the 1930s, the federal government acted to protect our culture from the overwhelming influence of the United States with the creation of the Canadian Radio Broadcasting Corporation, which later became the CBC. It did things that private radio, with its attention to the bottom line rather than a mandate to promote a national culture, could or would not do. By the late 1950s, television had been added to the CBC's power as Canadians enjoyed not just *Hockey Night in Canada*, but also Canadian news and entertainment.

Another product of the 1930s and of the federal government's seeking to further bolster our cultural sovereignty and national identity was the National Film Board (NFB). Created in 1939, the NFB had 787 full-time staff by 1945, which made it the world's largest film studio. In the 1950s, the NFB was rendered independent of government control, its head office was moved to Montreal, and its role broadened to create films that portrayed Canada not just to Canadians, but also to the world. By the 1960s, more francophone, Aboriginal, and women filmmakers were given access to funds, equipment, and training. A wider range of stories were told.

The NFB later expanded into regional centres, and films for television and theatrical release continued to be well made and received. Kids were exposed to their country and fellow Canadians through the clicking of 8-mm NFB films in their classrooms. The NFB's international reach was seen with its winning its first Academy Award in 1941 for a film on Churchill Island. It went on to earn nearly 70 nominations and win 11 more Oscars.

In 1951, the federal government received a Royal Commission report suggesting ways in which it could lead more efforts to bolster our culture. The Massey Report noted, for instance, that in the year of its study Canadian authors published only 14 books of English-language fiction. The challenge was accepted and the government partnered with Sir James Dunn and Izaak Walton Killam to create and fund the Canada Council for the Arts. It reported to cabinet, but its board acted at arm's length from the government. Peer assessment panels were established to consider grant applications from artists in a host of endeavours. Soon the national government's initiative and funding allowed talented Canadians who would have otherwise been rendered silent, due to their inability to make a reasonable living, to add voices to the chorus of those celebrating and adding nuance to what it meant to be Canadian.

Canadian music has a long and rich history. While Pierre Trudeau was running for office in 1968 there were thriving music scenes in Toronto, Winnipeg, Vancouver, and Halifax, but what had been true for decades remained the case — there was no Canadian music industry. There were few recording studios and those that existed were substandard. There were few Canadian record companies. As a result, nearly the only Canadians heard on Canadian radio were those such as Paul Anka, who had sought a career in the United States.

Radio station managers used American music charts such as *Billboard* magazine's to determine their playlists. Even venues such as the iconic Canadian National Exhibition and Calgary Stampede hired American and not Canadian bands to headline their shows. That all changed with the action of the federal government.

In 1968, the Broadcasting Act created the Canadian Radio-television Commission (CRTC), which was renamed the Canadian Radio-television and Telecommunications Commission in 1976. The CRTC's founding chairman, Pierre Juneau, was an unapologetic nationalist who acted under the auspices of the secretary of state to establish and enforce regulations that determined the percentage of Canadian content that had to make up everything broadcast over Canadian television and radio. AM radio stations, the primary source of music at the time, were told that starting in January 1971 their licences would depend upon 30 percent of all the music they played being Canadian. To be considered Canadian, at least two categories of the music, lyrics, production, or recording had to be done by Canadians.

Private radio stations protested to the CRTC and to the government, but they were given no quarter. Almost overnight, a Canadian music industry was born. Emerging acts such as The Guess Who and Gordon Lightfoot found a far more receptive Canadian market for their songs. Studios were built. New Canadian record labels scrambled to sign and record acts that had been scraping by in smoky little clubs and bars. Many created hit songs and high school kids loved the fact that their favourite band, be it Lighthouse, Edward Bear, or April Wine, had a hit on the radio but was also playing in their town. Just as the federal support of writers, playwrights, and filmmakers was doing, federal CRTC regulations allowed Canadians to appreciate that our stories and perspectives have value and that art is not something created only by foreigners. Pierre Juneau and the essential role played by the federal government in helping Canadians hear Canadian songs is remembered each year when the best in Canadian music earns the coveted Juno Award.

PATRIATION

Part of the enormously negative reaction to the National Energy Program was based on the fact that it arrived at the same time Trudeau was trying to make good on his promise to rejig Canadian federalism and bring home the Constitution. Shortly after the Quebec referendum results were announced, he dispatched cabinet ministers to provincial capitals, as he had in 1970, to again see exactly what the premiers wanted in return for the Constitution's patriation. He understood that since 1927 every attempt to move nation building forward a step by gaining Canadian control of the Canadian Constitution had been blocked by provincial demands to betray Sir John's vision by shifting power from Ottawa to them. The new provincial consultations informed Trudeau that it would happen again. He determined that this time the federal government would defeat provincial intransigence.

Trudeau proposed a two-stage process. They would begin with negotiations about a people's package — a charter of rights. They would then negotiate a politician's package — an altered division of powers between the federal and provincial governments that included the elusive formula for future constitutional amendments. It sounded easy. It wasn't. Lougheed was in the middle of an oil war. Lévesque was still smarting from his referendum loss. All premiers were fighting economic hardships and gnashing teeth over social program expenses and administrative responsibilities that had seemed reasonable when agreed to in better times. It would be another battle over a vision of Canada. Lougheed and Lévesque knew what side they were on. The premiers looked for a vision to embrace, alliances to forge, and enemies to fight.

A good deal of negotiating went on behind closed doors. The premiers had agreed among themselves on a list of 10 powers they wanted shifted to them in order to agree to patriate the Constitution and then another 10 that would be transferred after it arrived home. Trudeau rejected the so-called Château Consensus. The premiers set the stage for the upcoming public meetings by proposing that Trudeau share the chair with one of them. He wouldn't fall for that. There was, he said, only one voice that could speak for Canada.

The formal meetings were set around a large table in Ottawa's Government Conference Centre, the old, ornate, high-ceilinged former train station across the street from the iconic Château Laurier hotel. Television allowed Canadians to watch the spectacle of men fighting for their country and collective future. Not since America's Watergate hearings had transfixed so many of us a few years earlier had so many people been glued to their screens following arcane constitutional debates. We watched each premier enunciate demands. Trudeau's poise was tested when Newfoundland's Brian Peckford said that given the choice between the prime minister's vision of Canada and Premier Lévesque's, he sided with Lévesque. It was a stunning declaration. No premier challenged one of their compatriots aligning himself with a man and vision determined to destroy the country. The conference ended with the battleground established but nothing of substance accomplished.

Trudeau reacted to the provincial intransigence by threatening to ignore the premiers and bring the Constitution home without their consent. He called British Prime Minister Margaret Thatcher who agreed that if the Canadian government requested the necessary British action to allow the Constitution's patriation then she would make it happen. Trudeau went on television and announced that if the premiers would not agree to reasonable terms, then Ottawa would move unilaterally to bring the Constitution home and include within it a charter of rights for Canadians.

Combative premiers from each province except Ontario and New Brunswick, dubbed the Gang of Eight, would not stand for that. The group sent representatives to London to urge British parliamentarians to reject Trudeau's requests for unilateral action. Members of the group published full-page ads in newspapers across the country that outlined new proposals for power shifts and the so-called Alberta amending formula. To stand in solidarity with the others, Lévesque had surprisingly agreed to drop Quebec's veto over future amendments. The Gang of Eight took its case to Newfoundland's Supreme Court, which led to its bouncing to Canada's Supreme Court.

The Supreme Court moved with unusual speed. In September 1981, the court decided that the federal government was within its rights to act on its own, but that such action would contravene convention. The Supreme Court also ruled that for the Constitution to be brought home, amended, and a charter attached, a "substantive" number of provinces should agree. No one knew and it didn't say what was meant by the word *substantive*. Ontario's Premier William Davis and New Brunswick's Premier Richard Hatfield publicly announced their support for Trudeau's goal and tactics.

Davis disagreed with Trudeau on nearly everything and fought unashamedly and well for Ontario's interests, but shared the prime minister's desire to patriate the Constitution and embed a charter. There were times, he had told his stubborn provincial colleagues in Victoria, when the national interest must take precedent over provincial desires and when a prime minister must finally decide. After the Victoria conference's failure, he spoke as few premiers ever had, and as Sir John would have dreamed of hearing, when he said, "I am a Canadian who lives and works in Ontario. It is not the other way around. The whole of Canada is always greater than the sum of its parts."[5] With the prime minister contemplating unilateral federal action, Davis travelled under the media's radar to Ottawa and in a private meeting urged Trudeau to meet with the premiers one more time. He threatened to withdraw Ontario's support if Trudeau refused.

Two months later, we flicked on our TV sets again to watch what promised to be a showdown on the Rideau Canal. Neither side would budge. The Gang of Eight insisted that Ottawa surrender to its power-shift package. The gang's members refused even to discuss a charter of rights until Trudeau agreed to all their demands. During a coffee break, Trudeau sidled up to Lévesque and suggested that since he was a great democrat and had offered Quebecers a referendum, then he should support a Canada-wide referendum on a new charter. Without consulting anyone, Lévesque agreed. He said he would welcome a charter fight.

Unwittingly, Lévesque had broken the Gang of Eight. The other premiers shuddered at the thought of going to their people and arguing against a charter of rights. Trudeau perhaps too gleefully gloated to the media about the new Ottawa-Quebec alliance. He told reporters that the cat was now among the pigeons. With the other nine provincial delegations staying at the Château Laurier, Lévesque and his people left for their hotel across the Ottawa River in Quebec. His lodging decision changed Canada's history.

Late at night, Trudeau's justice minister, Jean Chrétien, met with Saskatchewan Attorney General Roy Romanow and Ontario Attorney General Roy McMurtry in a tiny fifth-floor convention centre pantry. On a page ripped from a notebook, they scratched out the details of a deal. They discussed a constitutional amendment to cede more federal power over resources to the provinces and provinces being able to opt out of federal programs but having to give up the related money. They agreed that equalization payments should be constitutionally entrenched. The Alberta amending formula should be adopted where change would require the consent of seven provinces constituting more than half Canada's population. But Quebec should be held to what Lévesque had offered and so there should be no Quebec veto on constitutional amendments. Most significantly, they agreed that the charter should be accepted if it included a notwithstanding clause specifying that under certain conditions a province could pass a law that contradicted charter rights applicable to fundamental freedoms, equality rights, and legal rights. The legislation would have to be revisited every five years and could not apply to the guaranteed rights of democracy, mobility, language, minority education, and gender equality. The three shook on the deal and set out to sell it.

Throughout the night one premier after another signed on. Manitoba's premier had returned home to campaign but was called and he agreed. After ten o'clock in the evening, Chrétien met Trudeau at the prime minister's Sussex Drive home. Trudeau quickly accepted the compromise terms but recoiled at the notion of weakening the charter with a not-withstanding clause. His first instinct was to scuttle it all and go back to the table or ignore the premiers altogether. Premier Davis then called, and in a 10-minute conversation told Trudeau that this was as good a deal as would be forth-coming. It was time to take it or leave it. Trudeau swallowed hard, reminded himself that politics is the art of the possible, and accepted that patriation would be won and that the char-ter he had championed for so long would be as well, even if somewhat watered down in order to avoid losing it all.

At breakfast the next morning, Lévesque could not believe what had happened. The Gang of Eight was now the Group of One. Without knowing what had happened over-night, Canadians tuned in the next day to watch a group of tired-looking men assemble around the great table. Lévesque steamed and smoked when Trudeau asked Newfoundland's Brian Peckford, who would later claim to have proposed and sold the deal, to read the agreement. Lévesque's scowl was deep and his rage scarcely hidden, but he clung to the hope that Trudeau would never agree. He was sincerely shocked when Trudeau announced that he would. The deal was made. Trudeau banged the gavel and only half joked that they should run before anyone changed his mind.

Lévesque was enraged. He stormed from the room red-eyed and sweating. With cigarette in hand and hair askew, he ignored how he had forgone strategy for tactics and thereby fumbled negotiations. Instead, he fumed at news cameras that Quebec had been cheated. Trudeau, he said, had "screwed" him.

On April 17, 1982, a large crowd gathered on Parliament Hill to watch their country be reborn. It was also celebrated in gatherings across the country. The signing of the new Canadian Constitution, the Canada Act, with its Charter of Rights and Freedoms was a big deal. On a windswept stage before the cheering crowd, the Queen signed. Trudeau added his name with such a flourish that he snapped the pen's nib. Her Majesty smiled as Justice Minister Chrétien muttered *"Merde"* and quickly scrambled for a pen to add his signature. Then, as if on cue, a drenching rainstorm blew in from Quebec.

Trudeau had used the power of the federal government to move Canada through the final steps of its independence from Britain. He had built upon the work of John Diefenbaker, who, in 1960, had created Canada's first Bill of Rights to secure a Charter of Rights and Freedoms that was more expansive and profound because it was not simply a piece of legislation, but part of our Constitution. The charter clearly defined how governments would work with one another and how Canadians would interact with them. Trudeau was happy to have the constitutional matters settled and the worms jammed back in the can once and for all. But they were pesky fellows. With the help of a well-meaning prime minister, they wiggled their way out. Then another prime minister tried to change them to snakes.

7

THE PROVINCIAL PHOENIX

All he was doing was fishing. In 1984, Ron Sparrow was arrested for using a net longer than Canadian law allowed. He was angry. A member of the Musqueam First Nation, Sparrow argued that his people had been fishing the Fraser River in British Columbia for thousands of years and that their right to do so was protected by treaty no matter what provincial or Canadian laws said. Sparrow's case eventually found itself at the Supreme Court. It was among the first to be decided according to the new Charter of Rights and Freedoms that Trudeau's determined efforts had included as part of Canada's patriated Constitution.

The court said Sparrow was right. It ruled that the law was inconsistent with Section 35's recognition and affirmation of existing Aboriginal treaty rights. Sparrow's arrest was overturned. The case was important, for it was among those inaugurating a new era in Aboriginal-establishment relations within Canada and because it demonstrated the enormous power the charter had placed with the Supreme Court. All federal and provincial laws and actions would now be seen through the charter's lens. Justices appointed by the prime minister, with no provincial consultation, were more formidable than ever before.

It was this power that premiers had feared in their years of fighting first against ending ties with the Judicial Committee of the Privy Council and then against a charter. It is why premiers had fought to weaken the charter and the justices with the inclusion of Section 33, the notwithstanding clause. They were trying to protect their power and legislative manoeuvrability even if it meant guaranteeing their right to limit our rights through the passage of laws that would violate them. But provinces seldom mustered the nerve to pull the notwithstanding clause trigger. A bitter Quebec legislature included a mention of Section 33 in every law it passed, whether applicable or not, until a new government was elected and stopped the silly, chest-thumping practice. Quebec's only real use of the clause came with its passage of a law restricting English on signs. Yukon invoked it once, but then did not proclaim the law to which it was attached. Saskatchewan used it to pass back-to-work legislation, but then discovered that its law didn't violate the charter, anyway. In 2000, Alberta used the clause to define marriage as the union of a man and a woman, but was told that it was a federal matter and so its law was scrubbed regardless of Section 33. The charter changed Canada by rendering the country a more constitutional nation as well as a parliamentary democracy and increased federal power by affording the federally appointed Supreme Court broader shoulders. But the dust on Section 33 suggests that while the provinces might not have liked it, they learned to accept it.

Upon returning to power, Pierre Trudeau had quipped, "Welcome to the 1980s." Although he welcomed us to the decade, it was his successor, after John Turner's two-month stint, that set the decade's post-patriation agenda.

Brian Mulroney took office in 1984 amid a devastating recession and the growing dominance of a right-wing, anti-government ideology sweeping the Western world. That sweep was seen with the election of Ronald Reagan in the United States in 1980. Having surveyed years of economic stagnation, cultural conflict, and the federal government's apparent inability to address either, Reagan famously said that government was not the solution to the problem, but the problem itself. U.K. Prime Minister Margaret Thatcher demonstrated similar beliefs with her attacks on trade unions and the partial dismantling of Britain's social welfare state.

A number of actions taken by Mulroney's government reflected the Reagan-Thatcher anti-government mindset. Those actions also announced that the new prime minister was unlike Trudeau, or Sir John for that matter, in his willingness to surrender federal power to the provinces. Those who believed in a more decentralized, provincially powerful Canada joined Albertans in applauding Mulroney's scrapping of the National Energy Program. They clapped again when Mulroney sold 23 Crown corporations, including Petro-Canada. He even oversaw the tearing up of railway tracks, the once-grand symbol of Canadian nationhood. Mulroney's perspective was also apparent in the attempt to relinquish even more federal power via the Meech Lake and Charlottetown accords.

And with that we are back. After 150 or so pages, we have returned to Prime Minister Mulroney attempting to right what he perceived as wrong about the 1982 constitutional agreement. Quebec had still not signed. Like Trudeau, Mulroney saw Canadian unity as among his greatest priorities. Also like Trudeau, he determined that the constitutional can of worms had to be reopened. But that is where they differed. Mulroney sought greater unity through the securing of Quebec's missing signature on the Constitution by offering a vision of Canada that was starkly different than Trudeau's. He believed the charter was too weak because of the notwithstanding clause and that empowering the Supreme Court had "Americanized" the country. His strongest objection was that it had been wrong to patriate the Constitution without Quebec's consent and argued that it would have been better to miss the moment and wait for a Quebec government more willing to sign on.[1]

The Supreme Court, meanwhile, had determined that the missing signature was meaningless. Quebec was a part of Canada, so the Constitution applied to it and its citizens as much as the document did to all other provinces, territories, and Canadians. However, the absence of Quebec's signature, as Mulroney correctly observed, had become a hot and glaring beacon for those seeking evidence to prove their belief that Ottawa was crazy with power and blind to Quebec's dignity, needs, and aspirations. Sovereignists exploited it as René Lévesque had portrayed it — a symbol of betrayal. Mulroney instituted a new round of negotiations with the provinces and then gavelled first ministers' meetings, behind closed doors this time, to change the eight-year-old Canada Act in ways that would seduce Quebec to sign. The premiers unshelved their old demands for the new talks.

Mulroney was brilliant in forging a complex agreement, but it failed in 1990 when Manitoba and Newfoundland refused to ratify the package of constitutional amendments called the Meech Lake Accord. Instead of giving up, over the next two years Mulroney and former prime minister and now Minister of Constitutional Affairs Joe Clark drank too much coffee and ate too many muffins in too many meetings as they negotiated yet another set of even broader constitutional amendments. The second try involved a much more open process. They celebrated when all ten premiers and both territorial leaders as well as four national committees and commissions, three Aboriginal organizations, and all major media outlets agreed that the new set of changes, the Charlottetown Accord, should be implemented. To cap an unprecedented consultation process, the accord's fate would be decided with a national referendum. Initial polls indicated that it would be overwhelmingly approved. It was a rare moment of unanimity in a country that seldom agrees on anything except hockey, beer, and winter.

Like the Meech Lake Accord, the Charlottetown Accord was created to shift considerable power to provincial governments. It gave provinces exclusive power to control mining and forestry. While Ottawa would still control the National Film Board and Canadian Broadcasting Corporation, the provinces were given exclusive power over cultural affairs. The accord reduced federal power over labour, training, immigration, and telecommunications by saying that provinces had to agree to any changes that might harmonize related processes or policies. Similarly, it said Ottawa needed provincial consent to use its constitutional power to claim jurisdiction over large infrastructure projects deemed to be to the "advantage of

Canada." But provinces could create their own programs, and as long as they met national standards, the federal government would have to pay its share of the funding. After a three-year waiting period, Aboriginal self-government would be recognized; Quebec would be immediately deemed a distinct society. The Supreme Court would need to consider both expressions of status when judging future federal actions. The power of the House of Commons would be reduced by making the Senate Triple-E. That is, it would become elected rather than appointed by the prime minister. It would be equal, with the same number of senators coming from each province. And it would become effective, so that House bills would die forever if opposed by a majority of senators, or, in some cases, a majority of francophone senators. The agreement would also abolish the seldom-used constitutional power to disallow provincial laws or dismiss provincial governments that acted against Canadian interests. Finally, the number of items in the Constitution that needed unanimous provincial support to be changed was increased, and any province could opt out of future constitutional amendments that appeared to shift power to the federal government.

Two things were obvious. Mulroney and Clark deserved top marks for winning the agreement of so many on so much. Second, the proposed power shift to provincial governments was titanic. Then it was all up to us. And the meetings and arguments began.

Canadians had lived through a generation of struggles over the Constitution and Quebec's place in the country. In the 1960s, separatist bombs had killed people. In 1970, a domestic terrorist group had kidnapped two politicians and killed one. In 1980, a Quebec referendum had nearly killed the country. Albertans and others in the western provinces, meanwhile, had become even more angry than usual with a federal government believed to be stuck in the mindset of thinking Canada consisted of the Toronto-Ottawa-Montreal triangle and everywhere else was just a region.

Some in the media expressed concern that too many people did not understand the complex Charlottetown Accord proposals laid before them and that others might just vote yes to put an end to all the constitutional and Quebec bickering. Early polls suggested the yes side was indeed winning. But then, as Prime Minister Diefenbaker once quipped, perhaps dogs are the only ones who know what to do with polls. Indeed, the consensus crumbled.

The turn began in a Montreal restaurant inelegantly called Maison Egg Roll. On a cool October 1, the gaunt and grey but still charismatic former prime minister Pierre Trudeau delivered a speech in which he called the Charlottetown Accord "a big mess." Trudeau opposed it for the same reason he had publicly fought Meech Lake with an impassioned appeal before a Senate committee. Despite the fact that some of the agreement's terms were similar to those he had advocated previous to patriation in 1982, Trudeau argued that the power shift to the provinces was unwise for Canadians and unnecessary for Quebecers. Those from his home province, he said, were already sufficiently protected by the charter and strong enough to stand on their own without what he viewed as the insulting symbolism of special status. Furthermore, he argued that the constitutional changes took so much power from Ottawa that it would become an emasculated "head waiter to the provinces." More important, he said, the accord would shift so much power from the centre that the centre might not hold. With the federal government no longer able to provide a national voice, the centrifugal provincial forces would inevitably lead to Canada flying apart.

The Egg Roll speech, as it became quaintly known, changed everything. Trudeau was arguing against the Canadian elite, popular opinion, and the dominant ideology of the day in insisting that primary political power should, and must legitimately and by practical necessity, rest with Ottawa. He afforded weight to others who were also opposing the accord, including Reform Party leader Preston Manning, who, ironically, was in opposition not because the accord shifted too much power to the provinces but because it did not shift enough. Trudeau, Manning, and others offered rallying points for those who were dubious about the accord on its merits, but also those who were against it just because the widely unpopular Mulroney was for it. Within a week of Trudeau's speech, support dropped 20 percent.

On October 26, 1992, a majority of Canadians (54.3 percent) and majorities in six provinces, including Quebec, voted no. The Meech Lake Accord, which proposed relocating power to the provinces, had been stillborn. With the referendum result, the Charlottetown Accord, which had tried to move even more power, was dead too.

No one can know the minds of folks who leaned over tables in church basements and school gyms to vote yes or no to a complicated set of constitutional amendments. However, no matter the myriad reasons for the accord's rejection, on that day we determined that Canada's future would be shaped more by the federal government than by provincial governments. In a mighty wave of democratic expression, we said the federal government spoke for us, and in so doing, for Canada.

❖

Like all things Canadian, things are not as simple as they seem. While Mulroney surrendered power through some of his policies and attempted to permanently cede more with his constitutional ideas, he was still willing to use that power for what he perceived as the good of the country. His use of federal power to build Canada's strength and unleash its potential was just as Sir John, that other great pragmatist, had intended. Consider the Mulroney government's actions with respect to the economy and the environment. Sir John would have opposed one and been confused by the other, but he would have applauded Mulroney's boldness.

Brian Mulroney took office when annual deficits had been growing for years and adding enormously to the national debt. The fiscal situation left little wiggle room for the federal government so, rather than play at the edges of the economy, Mulroney took audacious steps to change the game. Much like R.B. Bennett did in the 1930s, Mulroney used Ottawa's power to restructure and redirect the economy. He did it through changing trade and taxes.

No one likes taxes, but we all need them. As U.S. Supreme Court Justice Oliver Wendell Holmes once observed, taxes are the price we pay for living in a civilized society. The Mulroney government brought Canada in line with most other developed countries in moving a class of taxes from businesses to consumers. In 1991, the old Manufacturer's Tax was replaced by the Goods and Services Tax (GST). The move was hugely unpopular and temporarily hurt the economy and people's pocketbooks. Economists generally agreed, however, that the modernizing move was overdue and would bring long-term benefits to people, business, and the federal government, which would collect more revenue than before. The new money could tackle the debt and deficit while allowing for more program spending.

Everyone likes fair and profitable trade, as it creates business opportunities for some and jobs for others. Everyone likes lower prices. No one likes it, though, when a trade deal benefits only a few and transports investment and jobs overseas while leaving suddenly unemployed people with cheaper goods they can no longer afford. Trade is a delicate dance between short-term pain and long-term benefits; what is good for some and for all; and what helps people, business, finance, regions, and the country's sovereignty.

Sir John came down on the side of high-tariff protectionism. Mulroney did not. Mulroney went where Laurier had trod and King had ventured but at the last minute retreated. He negotiated a complex free trade agreement with the United States. The reaction was explosive. A number of premiers, union leaders, and business executives acknowledged the long-term benefits promised through the creation of even closer links with the world's largest market, but also noted the devastating short-term effects of unfettered American competition. The fight was played out in the 1988 election. It led to one of the most dramatic moments in televised campaign debates when Liberal leader John Turner tore into the prime minister with accusations of selling out Canada. An effective Liberal TV commercial showed the Canadian-American border as a pencil line being slowly erased. As in 1911, the election became a quasi-referendum on free trade. This time, however, Mulroney's Progressive Conservatives were re-elected with another majority government. The free trade agreement came into effect in January 1989. The slow and often painful transition brought about by a federal government convinced of the eventual benefits of the deal began.

Mulroney was not through. Working with Mexican and American leaders, the North American Free Trade Agreement (NAFTA) was negotiated over a number of years and over the objections of many Canadian consumer and business groups and provincial premiers. He again argued that he was doing what was in the best long-term interests of the country despite the fact that it would add to the rocky transition period toward freer trade in an increasingly globalized economy. He promised that "side deals" were still being negotiated, and they would alleviate some concerns. Mulroney knew that his personal popularity would suffer, as it had with the GST and the U.S. free trade agreement, but he told Canadians and those in his nervous caucus that the role of the national government is not to do what is popular, but what is beneficial for the country. NAFTA came into effect shortly after Mulroney left office.

The modern environmental movement was born with the 1962 publication of Rachel Carson's *Silent Spring*. It took a long time for us to catch up. When finally pushed by Canadian environmental groups, it was the federal government, with its capacity to act, that accepted the challenge to do so. For too long, environmental protection and economic growth were accepted as a choice by those unwilling to consider the seriousness of the problem or the price of solutions. The Trudeau government took tentative steps toward ending the false choice by creating a number of national parks. Mulroney, though, took two major leaps forward.

The first came with the passage of the 1988 Environmental Protection Act. The provinces were aghast. Canadian law acknowledged that resources were a provincial responsibility, but determined that because the environment does not recognize borders, environmental protection must also ignore imaginary provincial lines. The law established national standards with respect to the manner in which companies operated. Traditionally, dirty players such as pulp-and-paper factories, for example, were given strict new pan-Canadian regulations regarding what they could discharge into the air and water. Most industries fought back and many provinces chaffed at the exertion of the federal government's power. Mulroney remained tough. Changes were made.

In 1990, Mulroney's government made regulations even stronger with the passage of the Canadian Environmental Assessment Act. Quebec led the provinces' negative reaction with a Supreme Court case arguing that the environment laws trampled on the provinces' power to control resources. Specifically, Quebec said the new Canadian law would negatively impact its enormous James Bay Project. The Supreme Court ruled that while resources were indeed within the provincial realm, the federal government's jurisdiction over criminal law gave it the power necessary to create and enforce environmental protection laws and regulations.

The Attorney General of Canada v. Hydro-Québec (1997) was a landmark case. It reminded everyone that the days of the London Lords siding with the provinces was over. It also provided another example of the federal government's power being used to promote a national agenda. While critics quite rightly noted the environmental compromises in the U.S. free trade agreement and NAFTA, especially with respect to U.S.

access to Canadian water, few questioned the appropriateness of Mulroney later winning international environmental awards and being dubbed Canada's greenest prime minister.

MULRONEY'S SHADOW

There was a contradiction at the heart of Mulroney's government. His legacy rests on his use of Ottawa's power to bring about fundamental changes to Canadian tax, trade, and environmental laws, but also on his desire to change the Constitution in ways that would have significantly hindered future federal governments' ability to be so bold. Another part of Mulroney's legacy was the long shadow he left with the coalition he forged to come to power in the first place. The coalition consisted of soft Quebec nationalists and aggrieved westerners wanting either a greater voice at Canada's table or the table smashed. Neither group was happy with progress made during the Mulroney years. Their frustration shattered the coalition and left angry determination in its place.

In his attempt to hold the tenuous and dangerous Quebec wing of the coalition together, Mulroney had brought Canada's former ambassador to France and Quebec nationalist Lucien Bouchard to his cabinet. Upset with the failure of the Meech Lake agreement, Bouchard quit and formed the Bloc Québécois, a Quebec-based separatist party. With the Parti Québécois fighting provincial battles, the Bloc represented Quebec interests in Ottawa, but its goal was the same: to have Quebec forge an independent state.

The western wing of Mulroney's coalition had begun to splinter even earlier. In the mid-1980s, Preston Manning, the son of a former Alberta premier, saw larger and larger audiences attracted to his argument that the federal government needed to be less intrusive in people's lives, more fiscally responsible, and more responsive to western needs. Many were attracted to the slogan "The West Wants In." The Reform Party of Canada was created in Winnipeg in 1987, based largely on Manning's ideas, western alienation, and a Reaganesque anti-government sentiment.

Mulroney stunted Reform's growth by doing as William Lyon Mackenzie King had done with similar challenges from upstart western parties. He appropriated their ideas. Every Reform Party candidate failed in the 1988 election. Its first member was elected in a 1989 by-election. Growing unease with Mulroney's use of the federal government's power and what was seen as pandering to Quebec, along with Manning's growing effectiveness, led greater numbers of disaffected right-wing Conservatives to wave Reform's flag.

With his coalition gone and his popularity sunk to unprecedented depths, Mulroney resigned in February 1993. In the election that October, the Progressive Conservative Party was crushed by the resurgent Liberals and anti-centralist parties Mulroney had inadvertently midwifed in Quebec and the West. While running candidates only in Quebec, Bouchard's new party elected 54 members of Parliament. It became Canada's not quite Loyal Opposition. The Reform Party surprised many by winning 52 seats with victories in Alberta, Saskatchewan, Manitoba, British Columbia, and even one in Ontario. A sad joke called the Progressive Conservatives the Corvette party — they only had two seats.

The 1993 election had more resonance than just the weariness of a recently departed prime minister too long in the saddle or the tendency of Canadians to occasionally throw the bums out. It signalled the insurgent power of a largely western-based party dedicated to reducing the federal government's power and a solely Quebec-based party whose goal was not just to reduce that power, but end it altogether. Sir John would have wept.

This turn of events poured gasoline on the emotional embers that glowed within those who had never surrendered René Lévesque's dream of a sovereign Quebec. A growing number of Quebecers took up the myth of Trudeau's 1982 constitutional betrayal and piled on the rejection of their aspirations in the failures of Meech Lake and Charlottetown. Among them was one of Lévesque's old lieutenants. Despite speaking English with a British accent and dressing as a British Lord, Jacques Parizeau was a long-serving and dedicated sovereignist who led the Parti Québécois to power and himself to the premier's office in 1994. He sincerely believed in Lévesque's interpretation of the failed 1980 referendum as an invitation to wait until next time. In Parizeau's mind, the next time was now. He organized Quebec's second sovereignty referendum for October 1995. His government pushed a bill through the legislature that outlined a new version of sovereignty-association. As in 1980, the campaign began quite well for the sovereignists, the yes side. When Parizeau and his team stumbled through a number of unforced errors, the charismatic Lucien Bouchard rushed home from Ottawa to take the campaign's reins. Polls said the yes side would win.

As Trudeau's justice minister, Jean Chrétien had played a major role in the 1980 referendum, so while he became prime minister with the Liberals' 1993 electoral victory, he was unpopular among many in his home province. Sovereignists branded him a sellout as vehemently as Albertans chided him for caring only about Quebec while sneering that the Liberal majority was based mostly upon its overwhelming seat count in Ontario. These factors, plus the recollection of Trudeau keeping his powder dry in 1980, led Chrétien and his ministers to remain relatively quiet during the referendum campaign, even as it appeared that the no side was losing.

Finally, on October 25, and for the first time in his mandate, Chrétien addressed Canadians on television. His tone was sombre and his message direct. He told Quebecers that they should not be fooled by what he called a trick question. He spoke of Canada's virtues and said that a yes vote was not an indication of a desire to negotiate with Canada but to leave Canada and risk a dangerous future.

On October 27, just three days before voting day, an estimated 100,000 enthusiastic patriots travelled from across the country to Montreal's Place du Canada/Dorchester Square. With songs and patriotic speeches, they urged Quebecers to remain in Canada. It was the largest rally in our history. People came not as provincial representatives, but as Canadians. Their national network, the CBC, carried the rally to their compatriots. Dubbed the Unity Rally, many Quebecers later confessed to having been moved by the presence of so many people who cheered, sang, and waved "*Non*" signs while passing a gigantic Canadian flag over their heads and around the square.

The vote result brought a razor-thin margin of difference. Only 50.58 percent of Quebecers voted to remain in Canada while 49.42 voted to leave. Parizeau quit and Bouchard left Ottawa to carry on the sovereignist fight as Quebec's premier. The Parti Québécois continued to govern and the Bloc

Québécois continued to send members to Ottawa, but the referendum loss demoralized the sovereignist movement.

The Chrétien government flexed Ottawa's muscles with the passage of the Clarity Act. It essentially stated that there would be no more referendums based on the complex, misleading questions of 1980 and 1995 and that a clear majority would need to indicate a desire to leave before action could be taken. The law showed that the federal government would not simply stand by while a province worked to sabotage what had been created at Confederation and then had been built by all Canadians. Quebec, naturally, fought the law all the way to the Supreme Court, but it was decreed that the federal government was within its rights to demand the clarity expressed in the law. Subsequent polls indicated that sovereignty's supporters were, over time, becoming mostly older white people who were not just a shrinking demographic, but literally dying off. The embers, however, glowed on.

As Quebec's sovereignist parties were flaming out, their western cousin was experiencing its own troubles. The same demographic changes that were hurting the BQ and PQ were damaging the Reform Party. Much of its support was based on increasingly minority views on social issues such as homosexuality, abortion, immigration, and women's rights. The party suffered and its legitimate ideas regarding western power and fiscal and constitutional reform were damaged every time a Reform supporter or party member said something that appealed to the party base but offended Canadians' sense of fairness and tolerance.

Chrétien's Liberals further stole the Reform thunder when, beginning in 1995, it instituted a program of restraint and budget cutting designed to eliminate the federal deficit.

Manning reminded Canadians that Ottawa was balancing its books on the backs of the provinces by cutting transfers to social programs that had begun with 50-50 cost-sharing agreements. Mulroney had begun the cuts to provinces, and premiers had reacted with a 1991 Supreme Court challenge. The court declared that the federal government was within its rights to control its spending, even if fiscal changes affected agreements it had signed with the provinces. The ruling did not stop premiers from protesting the new round of cuts, but, like Mulroney, Chrétien stuck to his plan and accomplished his fiscal goals. In 1996, the two avenues through which Ottawa supplied money to the provinces were replaced by the Canada Health and Social Transfer, and provinces quickly screamed that the overall funding was nearly $2 billion less than promised.

The cuts to provinces led Ontario and Alberta to argue, at the annual premiers' conference in 1995, that the federal government should just pull out of social programs altogether. The other provinces disagreed. Quebec said nothing, since it was boycotting the conference. The premiers got their act together in 1998 and unanimously asserted that Ottawa should stop cutting program spending and should not be allowed to begin any new social programs without their unanimous consent. Prime Minister Chrétien replied only that the premiers should stick to their provincial concerns and that if they wanted to govern Canada, then they should run for federal office.[2] Soon, and for the first time in decades, the Canadian government enjoyed a budgetary surplus. Provinces and municipalities painfully adjusted to the new era of fiscal federalism, and the long-established social programs that had come to define our citizenship carried on. Canadians continued to pay for them simply by taking more money from one pocket and less from the other.

The new federal-provincial squabbling played to the Reform Party's advantage. It sung its anti-Ottawa tune through the 1997 election and formed the Official Opposition. The fact that all of its 60 seats were from the west led many to wonder about the party's future. Manning realized that the party's anti-Quebec, anti-progressive, anti-centralist, anti-Ottawa, and libertarian policies were relegating its support to a regionally based, socially conservative, dwindling few. He organized meetings across the country that, in 2000, eventually led to the formation of the Canadian Alliance Party. Its anti-Ottawa stance was as firm as the Reform Party's had been, but its rhetoric was more measured. It didn't matter. From the rolling thunder of Reform's ideas came a storm that shook the country.

THE HARPER MOMENT

Jean Chrétien led the Liberal Party to a third majority victory in November 2000. The rare electoral feat by the pro-centralist Chrétien was impressive, but everyone knew his success was partially due to his opposition being divided among the still small Progressive Conservatives and the regionally based Alliance Party and Bloc Québécois. The three-way split allowed Chrétien's view to prevail, but it could not mask that a significant number of Canadians continued to believe that the federal government was too strong and intrusive and beholden to central Canadian money and perspectives — and for many Quebecers, the old Anglo oligarchs. Some spoke of the long-standing, sherry-sipping, power-loving,

Montreal-Ottawa-Toronto-based Laurentian elite. The University of Calgary became a centre for dissenters fired up by those ideas and disgruntled Western thought that resented everything the Laurentian elite represented. Among their number was Stephen Harper.

Harper was born and grew up in Ontario, but he quit university to move west and work in Imperial Oil's Calgary mailroom. As a serious, intelligent, and respected policy analyst and political strategist, Harper won election as a member of the Reform Party. Unhappy with what he perceived as Manning compromising principle for growth in the attempt to shift Reform from movement to party, Harper resigned. He returned to Calgary and became an influential member of the National Citizens Coalition, an advocacy group formed in 1967 to promote free enterprise and personal freedom through shrinking the power of government. He eventually became the libertarian organization's president.

Under the auspices of the National Citizens Coalition, Harper oversaw the composition of a January 2001 open letter to Alberta's Progressive Conservative Premier Ralph Klein. Signed by Harper and five other Calgary School conservatives, the letter was published in a number of newspapers across the country. It demanded that Alberta withdraw from the Canadian Pension Plan and form its own. Klein should let the RCMP contract lapse, then form a provincial force because the federal police treats Alberta like, "a laboratory for experiments in social engineering."[3] Alberta should pull out of the Canadian health-care program and form its own. To finance its new independence, Alberta should start collecting provincial sales taxes. Klein should also lead a national charge to re-open the Constitution to force the adoption of a

Triple-E Senate. Finally, the letter urged Klein to reduce the amount of tax that Albertans "send" to Ottawa and, through equalization payments, see transferred to poorer provinces. The letter concluded: "It is imperative to take the initiative, to build firewalls around Alberta, to limit the extent to which an aggressive and hostile federal government can encroach upon legitimate provincial jurisdiction."[4] It became known as the Firewall Letter. It stood Sir John's vision of Canada on its head.

Harper and the other authors hoped that Klein would act on the advice, but also that it would spark a groundswell of anti-Ottawa sentiment in the West and possibly across the country. People would rise up and demand greater power and independence for the provinces and end the federal government's use of its power to manipulate economic and social change. But they were wrong. Klein and Canadians ignored the Firewall Letter. It nonetheless remains important for the degree to which it revealed Harper's mission and helps us to understand his tenure as prime minister and see the dogged resilience of Sir John's vision.

With help from his Calgary friends, Harper used his Firewall Letter and anti-centralist, libertarian reputation to the win the leadership of the old Reform Party, the Canadian Alliance. In October 2003, the Progressive Conservative Party was swallowed by the Canadian Alliance to form the new Conservative Party of Canada. The next spring, Harper was chosen as its leader. His mandate was to unite the divided right and beat the Liberals. In fact, Harper had told friends and colleagues that he wished to see the Liberal Party not just defeated but erased from the Canadian political landscape. Liberals were not opponents. They were enemies. In Harper's mind, they were the embodiment of the Laurentian elite and pro-centralist perspective he was determined to destroy.

Meanwhile, Jean Chrétien's former finance minister, Paul Martin, had become prime minister. Martin's father, Paul Martin, Sr., had been a long-serving and influential cabinet minister who had worked closely with Lester Pearson in the 1960s to create and augment Canada's social safety net. With the federal government's deficit gone and the debt shrinking, Prime Minister Martin proposed a progressive agenda that would have swelled his father's chest. It was based on the belief that the federal government was a positive force to improve lives.

The Martin government undertook negotiations with the provinces to create a national daycare program. After years of Canadians seeing the federal government take no bold initiatives, polls indicated great support for the first new national program of its kind in a generation. It was based on other programs that had provinces sharing costs and handling administrative duties while enforcing national standards. Every premier signed on with the conviction that the program would reduce costs for families, promote greater safety and early education for children, and enable more women who wanted to work outside the home to do so. But it was not to be.

The minority Martin government was defeated in the House, due not to its strong pan-Canadian stances, as seen in its national daycare program or its announced plans to improve Aboriginal education, but mostly because of a spending scandal left over from the Chrétien years. In a rare winter election, Canadians replaced a minority Liberal government with a minority Conservative government in early 2006.

Stephen Harper would hold office for nearly a decade. He did not bring, as some claimed, a hard-right agenda. Indeed,

Harper refused to even discuss many of the social issues that right-wing folks yearned to have re-addressed in an attempt to undo the 1960s and 1970s, such as abortion and capital punishment. Rather, the guiding notion of his tenure was the anti-centralist power perspective so clearly stated in his Firewall Letter. Ironically working beneath a portrait of Sir John on his office wall, Harper set forth with a strategic goal to silence the old man's voice by emasculating the federal government and ensuring that his successors would be unable to restore what he had destroyed.

The first indication of Harper's anti-centralist strategy in practice was the elimination of Martin's national daycare program. It was replaced by monthly $100 cheques to parents. Harper said parents were better able to spend the money than the government and that there would be less wasteful spending if bureaucracies were not administering the national program. Parents accepted the cheques, of course, but with the understanding that the money covered the cost of only about four or five days of a month's daycare expenses. Paul Martin reacted with understandable dismay, saying, "What if, decades ago, Tommy Douglas and my father and Lester Pearson had considered the idea of Medicare and then said, 'Forget it! Let's just give people twenty-five dollars a week'? You want a fundamental difference between Mr. Harper and myself? Well, this is it."[5] Indeed, the difference spoke to their contrary visions of Canada; only one believed that Canada's government was a force for good.

It is significant that Prime Minister Harper was not just killing a national program to which provinces had already signed on, but also continuing to shovel money out the door. The national program would have ensured that the federal government's money would be spent on daycare. Parents, however, were free to spend their $100 on whatever they wished. The same surrender of Ottawa's influence with continued spending came when Harper told provinces that he would maintain the funding level that Martin had pledged for health-care costs until 2016. Except, where Martin had ensured the money would be spent in certain ways and maintain national standards, Harper removed those guarantees. Harper was not just ending the federal government's influence, but emptying its coffers.

The actions on daycare and health care must be seen in concert with Harper's introduction of a 2 percent cut to the Goods and Services Tax. Harper said it was good economics to leave money in the pockets of Canadians rather than to bring it to Ottawa to be wasted. Economists decried the move as doing little for Canadians or the economy, but they missed the point. The cut had nothing to do with economics. It would reduce revenue by about $12 billion a year. That was the point. Harper knew that his successors would find it exceptionally difficult to restore the higher GST rates after they had fallen. He was ensuring that future federal governments, already robbed of the business tax that Mulroney had ended, would have far less money from the GST that had replaced it. As with the daycare and health-care actions, the Firewall Letter's author was again demonstrating that he saw the federal government as a beast and that the best way to weaken it was to remove its teeth and food. Harper was not done. He attacked its brain.

Besides money and the strings attached to it, in order to operate programs and contemplate new ones, the federal government needs reliable information. Harper acted to stifle its flow. He ended the long-form census and drastically cut

Statistics Canada. It was claimed that too many Canadians were complaining that the long-form census violated their privacy, but no one seemed able to find out just who these Canadians were or if indeed anyone had complained at all. Harper also cut budgets to nationally funded scientific research programs and banned scientists from speaking with the media about their work. Meanwhile, Harper denigrated those who sought to base policies or even opinions upon statistics and facts. In April 2013, for example, Liberal leader Justin Trudeau suggested that the government should seek to better understand the root causes of terrorism and influences that radicalize youth. Prime Minister Harper dismissed the notion, saying, "This is not the time to commit sociology."[6]

Killing the daycare program, shovelling unfettered money to the provinces, cutting the GST, ending the long-form census, and gagging science, scientists, and intellectual discussion had the effect of crippling the federal government, starving it, and lobotomizing it. Harper had been unable to persuade Premier Klein to build a firewall around Alberta. As prime minister, he was building a firewall around Ottawa.

Harper's moment was jarring, but like all moments, it ended. In 2015, a renewed Liberal Party, led by Pierre Trudeau's son, and the New Democratic Party, which had, for the first time in its existence, become the Official Opposition, led a two-pronged attack on Harper's vision of Canada. Both Justin Trudeau and NDP leader Tom Mulcair spoke of a re-engaged federal government. They promised national programs to address long-festering national concerns. Harper countered with promises of more boutique tax cuts and hinted at dividing Canadians according to religious practices and whether or not they were "old-stock Canadians." All the while he sneered at the notion of new pan-Canadian initiatives. Despite having led it for nearly a decade, Harper spoke of the federal government as inefficient and wasting Canadians' money.

As with every time Canadians mark a ballot, a number of factors swirl in the decision-making and one must be careful in reading their minds. However, the results were clear. About 60 percent of Canadians voted for the NDP and Liberal vision of the country and only 32 percent supported Harper's view. Canadians elected a majority Liberal government selling a pan-Canadian, activist vision that the old Conservative, Sir John, would have applauded.

THE FUTURE

Upon settling into the prime minister's office, Justin Trudeau began tearing down the firewall Harper had been construct-ing. The long-form census was re-established. Money flowed again to research scientists, and they were encouraged to speak freely. Taxes were increased on the wealthy. Trudeau also did something Harper had done but once, and only for an informal dinner: he met with the premiers and spoke of a national vision for the country. In the summer of 2016, the federal government negotiated with the provinces to make substantive changes to the Canada Pension Plan. Workers and businesses were asked to begin contributing a little more in order to improve benefits in the light of the shrinking number of Canadians with defined pension plans. The federal govern-ment was back in the nation-building business.

It was also back in the business of crisis response. The fall of 2015 and spring of 2016 brought hard times to Alberta. In an April 2016 speech, Alberta Premier Rachel Notley spoke of the devastating impact of the sudden and dramatic collapse of world oil prices. It had resulted in the loss of more than 110,000 Alberta jobs. Notley said that just two years earlier, one-fifth of the Alberta government's revenue, some $10 billion, had come from oil and gas revenue. That revenue stream had fallen by 90 percent. She admitted that in the ten boom years previous to the collapse, the Alberta government and oil sector leaders had spoken of economic diversification to mitigate the next, inevitable crash, but nothing of substance had been done. The province remains, she confessed, "dangerously dependent on the price of oil."

Alberta needed help. Ottawa had already changed employment insurance rules to allow more money to flow to unemployed Alberta workers. The premier urged the prime minister to make more changes so even more people could access relief easier and longer. But then, biting the hand from which she was asking to be fed, Notley castigated Prime Minister Trudeau for his climate-change pledges and plans. She also urged him to immediately approve the Northern Gateway Pipeline from Alberta to the Pacific Ocean. It was an interesting turn, as during the campaign that brought her party to power, Notley had said that she opposed the pipeline and would not lobby for it. Continuing, and even more surprisingly, she issued a thinly veiled threat: "We can't continue to support Canada's economy, unless Canada supports us."[7]

As if Alberta's economic calamity was not enough, massive wildfires then visited destruction on a large area around the centre of Alberta's oil sands project at Fort McMurray. Nearly 90,000 people fled their homes. The province that had fought the federal government for so long and given birth to the

Reform Party, the Calgary School, and the Firewall Letter — and whose premier had so recently threatened to end support for the Canadian economy — needed Ottawa's help yet again.

Prime Minister Trudeau reacted with the compassion and decisiveness that a national leader should display. Over $30 million was matched with citizen donations and then funnelled to Alberta as efforts were coordinated with the province, the Red Cross, and other relief agencies to get water, food, cots, and more to where it was needed most. Trudeau assured Albertans that the federal government, and through it, all Canadians, were there for them and that there was no cap on the money and other support needed to address the emergency.

A perhaps even clearer indication that Prime Minister Trudeau was embracing Sir John's vision of federal power came in late 2016. For nearly 20 years, the Chrétien, Martin, and Harper governments had talked about battling climate change, but had done little about it. Their inaction led some provinces to move on their own to address the 21st century's principal challenge. Without federal leadership, however, the efforts were piecemeal and largely ineffective. Some provincial leaders continued to argue that there was no need to take substantive action because Canada was a minor contributor to the greenhouse gases that were causing global temperatures to rise while others clung to the hoary, false choice of either embracing environmental sustainability or economic prosperity. The voices were akin to those who had maintained that Canada could play only a small role in the global effort to combat Nazi Germany and that the effort would be expensive so it would be acceptable to turtle and do nothing. Fortunately, as in the Second World War, the best among us strove for better.

Among them was Prime Minister Justin Trudeau. In April 2016, he joined more than 50 other world leaders in signing the United Nations Framework Convention on Climate Change, more commonly called the Paris Agreement. Its goal was to combat climate change by keeping this century's global temperature rise less than 2°C above pre-industrial levels while helping those most directly impacted by the floods, storms, desertification, and other effects already occurring. All signatories promised to implement "nationally determined contributions" to pursue the agreement's goals and to report regularly on their greenhouse gas emissions reductions and other efforts. Trudeau pledged that Canada would join the global effort by cutting its emissions by 30 percent of 2005 levels by the year 2030.

Because the provinces control resources, many of which cause greenhouse gas emissions through the burning of carbon-based material, Trudeau needed them to join in the grand national effort. They needed to eliminate dirty sources of energy production, like coal, impose a price on carbon, essentially a tax, or introduce a cap-and-trade system in which emitters exceeding an established limit could buy credits from those under the limit. The point was made increasingly clear that we were not really trying to save the planet, for it would carry on no matter what we did. Rather, we needed to save ourselves and our posterity. Despite the evidence, options, urging, and impending crisis, however, some provinces made it clear they were not interested. Others proposed to play the crisis against demands for more federal health-care funding. It was again time for the cat-herding of federal leadership.

In October 2016, Trudeau stood in the House of Commons and announced that each province would need to reduce its carbon footprint, and "if neither price nor cap and trade is in place by 2018, the Government of Canada will implement a price in that jurisdiction."[8] He said the federal government would meet Canada's Paris pledge by imposing a $10 per tonne price on carbon dioxide pollution in 2018 that would increase by $10 per year until it reached $50 per tonne in 2022. The changes would entice market forces to reduce emissions. Trudeau promised that any revenue earned by the plan would be returned to the provinces from which the revenue was generated.

Provincial reaction was predictable. Ontario, Quebec, and British Columbia already taxed carbon or had cap-and-trade schemes in place and so praised the prime minister's leadership and spoke only of adjusting their targets. Others balked. Nova Scotia, Newfoundland and Labrador, and Saskatchewan walked out of a meeting with Canada's environment minister. Saskatchewan's Premier Brad Wall said, "The level of disrespect shown by the prime minister and his government today is stunning."[9] In fact, the only thing Trudeau was disrespecting were provincial leaders who were refusing to join him on the right side of history. Trudeau was respecting us by harnessing the power of the federal government as it was meant to be used, this time to turn the threat of climate change into a national challenge and opportunity. The deal was made in December 2016 and agreed upon by every province except Saskatchewan, which disagreed in principle, and Manitoba, which wanted to swap its signature for more health-care funding. The climate deal was both nation building and crisis response.

Trudeau's name reminded people of his father's vision of the country. His promise of seeking "sunny ways" to solve intractable problems reminded them of Wilfrid Laurier's commitment. The early actions of his administration were reminiscent of Sir John's concept of a strong federal government speaking for Canadians and with the power, data, capacity, and intention to act as a force for the national, collective good. It was evidence that the vision had survived the decentralizing provincial phoenix that had risen in Brian Mulroney's shadow and Stephen Harper's moment. There were indications that increasing numbers of people were fed up with provincial and regional politicians urging Canadians to think parochially within a globalized world. They had had enough of premiers and even a prime minister who ignored, belittled, or shunted aside a national common purpose.

Sir John and Canada's other founders understood that for a country to grow and flourish it must have a strong central core. In a federal system such as Canada's, power must be shared with the provinces and they must responsibly meet their obligations, but primary power must remain with the national government. Through this power balance, Sir John said, Canada would avoid the mistakes of the Americans, who placed too much power with the states. Sir John could not have guessed the challenges ahead, but his words and actions demonstrated his confidence that locating power in Parliament and with the national government would afford Canada the tools needed to meet anything tomorrow might bring. It would allow Canada to remain united in its complexity and determined in its common purpose.

The location of predominant power with the national government has indeed allowed the federal government to employ its constitutional, fiscal, and moral capacity to undertake nation-building endeavours. Examples include physical manifestations such as the transcontinental railway, St. Lawrence Seaway, and Trans-Canada Highway. They also include institutions such as the Bank of Canada, the National Film Board, the CRTC, and the CBC. Furthermore, they include expressions of community and citizenship seen most clearly in pensions, unemployment programs, health care, and the Charter of Rights and Freedoms. To varying degrees and in various ways, provincial governments fought each of these nation-building ventures. They came to fruition only through national leaders who spoke not to parochial interests, but to a national vision. They spoke for a belief in what was best not for those in a particular province or region, but for us all.

It is equally clear that Sir John's placement of paramount power with the national government allowed it to act as the country's first responder. It addressed crises that cities and provinces fumbled or could not reasonably handle on their own. The many examples include actions taken to fight world wars, the ravages of the Great Depression, and the 2015 oil-price crash. They also include reacting to emergencies as diverse as the 1919 Winnipeg General Strike, the 1970 kidnappings in Montreal, and the 2016 fires in Fort McMurray. In these and other crises, the federal government demonstrated its capacity to react and its ability to reflect the generosity of Canadians uniting as a national community.

Canada is a conversation. It is a never-ending conversation with ourselves about ourselves. It is about who we are and who we aspire to be. The conversation takes place in our songs, stories, paintings, poetry, and architecture. It is vibrantly expressed in loud bars at night, busy coffee shops each morning, and in sunlit parks where parents feel safe watching their children at play. The conversation is in the bluster of House of Commons table pounding, in backroom compromises and principled stands, and the rough and tumble of campaigns that are the messy but essential business of our democracy. Through it all, in public spaces and private places, the Canadian conversation creates transformational moments that affect us all.

Sir John established Canada's power arrangement to allow the civil and civic society conversations not to be splintered into parochial shards of narrow concerns, but rather to be reflected in national imperatives for the common good. British Lords tried to change it, provinces fought to tilt it, Quebec sovereignists sought to end it, and even a prime minister or two tried to sabotage it. But the power balance has always swung back to Sir John's founding vision. Always.

The 21st century has proven that history is not quite dead. Too many around the world have fallen into the black tar pit of nativism and racism, with individuals, groups, and entire countries finding it exceptionally hard to extract themselves after jumping in or even after dipping a toe into the hateful, paranoid muck. Canadians have had a first-row seat in watching America dance at the edge due to its inexplicable inability to move beyond the race war of the 1860s or cultural war of the 1960s. We watched the testing of its soul in the cacophony of folks shouting past one another in ideological screaming matches disguised as democratic debate. Canada is not immune. We have turned the desperate from our shores, locked up or kidnapped those of a race deemed unworthy or suddenly the enemy, and, sadly, much more for which we share justifiable shame. We have more recently considered dividing ourselves according to religion or cultural practices rather than celebrating the strength of our diversity. Down that road lies the pit.

Fortunately, Sir John and the founders created for us the perfect instrument to avoid the perils of divisions created by false assumptions, fears, and bogeymen invented by the cynically ambitious or know-nothing demagogues. The national government has the power and, in the right hands, the capacity to unite rather than divide through encouraging us all to see ourselves as Canadians. It has the ability to remind us that we are not just taxpayers or consumers or members of whatever group affords us comfort, but, rather, we are citizens. We are citizens by choice and by law and not by blood. While provinces tend to matters of importance, it is the federal government that allows that citizenship to be expressed with a national, unified, and unifying voice. It is a voice in rich harmony, but one voice. It is the national government's ability to unite that keeps us from the pit. It is the national government that deserves respect despite its flaws, past mistakes, and the necessary messiness of its democratic processes.

We can feel secure, happy, and proud that we have a strong voice in one of the oldest, safest, richest, and most stable countries the world knows or has ever known. Our voice is that of the federal government. When it speaks for us and for Canada, it's always with a hint of a soft Scottish burr, for it is, after all, Sir John's echo.

NOTES

CHAPTER 1: THE FOUNDERS' INTENTIONS

1. J.M.S. Careless, *Brown of the Globe, Volume 2, Statesman of Confederation 1860–1880* (Toronto: Dundurn, 1989), 181.

2. Donald Creighton, *The Road to Confederation: The Emergence of Canada 1863–1867* (Toronto: Macmillan Canada, 1964), 145.

3. P.B. Waite, *The Confederation Debates in the Province of Canada, 1865* (Toronto: McClelland & Stewart, 1963), 44.

4. Richard Gwynn, *Nation Maker: Sir John A. Macdonald; His Life, Our Times* (Toronto: Random House Canada, 2011), 71.

5. J.M. Beck, ed., *The Shaping of Canadian Federalism: Central Authority or Provincial Right?* (Toronto: Copp Clark, 1971), 163.

6. Peter W. Hogg, *Canadian Federalism, the Privy Council and the Supreme Court: Reflections on the Debate about Canadian Federalism* (Toronto: Osgoode Hall Law School of York University, Osgoode Digital Commons, 2005), 342.
7. Gwynn, *Nation Maker*, 379.
8. Geoffrey Perret, *Ulysses S. Grant: Soldier and President* (New York: Random House, 1997), 408.

CHAPTER 2: THE GREAT WAR

1. Tim Cook, *Warlords: Borden, Mackenzie King, and Canada's World Wars* (Toronto: Allen Lane, 2012), 62.

CHAPTER 3: THE CRASH

1. House of Commons Debates, May 6, 1930.
2. Ibid.
3. J.R.H. Wilbur, ed., *The Bennett New Deal, Fraud or Portent?* (Toronto: Copp Clark, 1968), 88.
4. House of Commons Debates, February 14, 1932.
5. Ibid., May 9, 1932.
6. R.C. Macleod and David Schneiderman, *Police Powers in Canada: The Evolution and Practice of Authority* (Toronto: University of Toronto Press, 1994), 46.
7. Ernest Watkins, *R.B. Bennett: A Biography* (Toronto: Kingswood House, 1963), 226.

CHAPTER 4: WAR AGAIN

1. Allan Levine, *King: William Lyon Mackenzie King: A Life Guided by the Hand of Destiny* (Vancouver: Douglas & McIntyre, 2011), 283.
2. House of Commons Debates, September 7, 1939.
3. William Lyon Mackenzie King, *Diaries*, September 25, 1939. Accessed at www.bac-lac.gc.ca/eng/discover/politics-government/prime-ministers/william-lyon-mackenzie-king/pages/item.aspx?IdNumber=20813.
4. Levine, *King*, 305.
5. Terry Reardon, *Winston Churchill and Mackenzie King: So Similar, So Different* (Toronto: Dundurn, 2012), 177.
6. Ibid., 135.

CHAPTER 5: CONCRETE AND COMMUNITY

1. John Boyko, *Bennett: The Rebel Who Challenged and Changed a Nation* (Toronto: Key Porter, 2010), 285.
2. Ibid., 289.
3. Tom Kent, *A Public Purpose: An Experience of Liberal Opposition and Canadian Government* (Montreal and Kingston: McGill-Queen's University Press, 1988), 269.

CHAPTER 6: RIGHTS AND RESOURCES

1. John English, *Just Watch Me: The Life of Pierre Elliott Trudeau, 1968–2000* (Toronto: Vintage Canada, 2010), 83.
2. Ibid., 90.
3. Pierre Elliott Trudeau, *Memoirs* (Toronto: McClelland & Stewart, 1993), 232.
4. Ibid., 290.
5. Steve Paikin, *Bill Davis: Nation Builder, and Not So Bland After All* (Toronto: Dundurn, 2016), 287.

CHAPTER 7: THE PROVINCIAL PHOENIX

1. Brian Mulroney, *Memoirs: 1939–1993* (Toronto: McClelland & Stewart, 2007), 510.
2. Garth Stevenson, "Federalism and Interprovincial Relations." In Michael Whittington and Glen Williams, eds., *Canadian Politics in the 21st Century* (Toronto: Nelson Thomson Learning, 2000), 95.
3. Open Letter to Ralph Klein, *National Post*, January 24, 2001.
4. Ibid.
5. Lawrence Martin, *Harperland: The Politics of Control* (Toronto: Viking Canada, 2010), 49.
6. Tobi Cohen, *National Post*, April 25, 2013.
7. Claudia Cattaneo, *National Post*, April 7, 2016.
8. Bruce Campion-Smith, *Toronto Star*, October 3, 2016.
9. Ibid.

ACKNOWLEDGEMENTS

Dividing and defining our village is a river that, as Lakefield resident Margaret Laurence once observed, runs both ways. It does, you know. It really does. It was on long, slow runs along the river that I wrote this book. Oh, certainly I typed it in my office, but the genuine work, the tumbling and juggling of ideas, the real stuff of writing, came accompanied by the falling of footsteps on the trail and the washing of water.

And so, odd as it may seem, I would like to acknowledge and thank the river for its uncaring but profound inspiration. It reminded me that somewhere beneath its gently flowing surface, at the heart of its magic, lies the metaphor for our country. The truth and what truly matters lie not in the surface sparkles, gleaming as diamonds in the sun, but with the rocks and roots and weeds below that roil all above, offering resistance and form. The river urged me to take a broader view; to consider more expansive ideas, deeper concepts; and to think not of passing fads and fancies that capture clicks and headlines, but what really matters. Power. The power to shape, inspire, speed up, or slow down, to move while lifting or, sometimes, pulling below.

That's what this book is all about. Power. It's the power of perpetual motion, of rugged beauty and gentle grace lying comfortably with the awful potential to direct or destroy. That is the river's power. That is Canada's power. That is the power we owe ourselves to contemplate: relentless power that moves even when we don't notice, while we sleep, flexed and expressed and occasionally challenged and while appearing to be heading in one direction in a natural, linear fashion, sometimes, flows both ways. I thank the river for encouraging my contemplation so that I might invite yours.

And what of Margaret Laurence? I thank her for being among those who taught me a love of words and a respect for the power of ideas powerfully expressed. There were others: Margaret Atwood, Leonard Cohen, John Lennon, Kurt Vonnegut, John Ralston Saul, John Prine, Doris Kearns Goodwin, Shelby Foote, Gwynne Dyer, Paul Simon, and John W. Boyko, Sr. I thank them all.

This book began with a conversation between Patrick Boyer, Steve Paikin, and me — three men insatiably entranced by books, politics, ideas, and Canada. Patrick invited me to contribute a book to Dundurn's Point of View series as part of a commemoration of Canada's 150th birthday. Make it controversial, Patrick urged, stir readers' passions and propose notions to spark debate. Thank you, Patrick, for inviting and trusting me to write and for your valuable suggestions on an early draft. I hope I have not let you down.

Thank you to the Dundurn team that embraced me so thoughtfully and supported me so professionally. I am grateful for the vision of president and publisher Kirk Howard, and for the editorial skills of Dominic Farrell, Cheryl Hawley, and Michael Carroll. I thank the talented Lawrence Martin for his constructive suggestions and fine foreword.

This is my seventh book, and I have lost count of the number of editorials, articles, and blog posts I have written. My dear wife, Sue, has read and edited every word. She brings to all I do an unparalleled editorial precision and skill and sense of when something is going on a little too long or needs to be fleshed out. She knows what it is about my work that works, and what doesn't. Her kindness, care, tenderness, wit, and love make all I do better, possible, and worthwhile.

I am grateful to Craig Pyette, Anne Collins, and Daphne Hart, who encouraged me in this project.

Being a father is one thing, but being a grandfather is something else altogether. Grandchildren teach you to love all over again. Without trying, my two sweet granddaughters remind me of all that truly matters, including the country in which they will be making their lives. Canada was not inevitable and is not immutable. All that is great about it, from its stunning physical beauty to the strength and marvel of its complexity, must be not just celebrated, but protected. You won't protect what you don't love and can't protect what you don't understand. Without understanding, we can sing about standing on guard, but not really do the deed. It is the future of my grandchildren, and yours, even if you don't yet know them, that makes striving to understand in order to protect what is worth protecting worthwhile. I thank my grandchildren for inspiring my contemplation of the home they deserve.

John Boyko
Lakefield, Ontario

Other Books by John Boyko

Cold Fire: Kennedy's Northern Front (2016)

Voisins et ennemis: la Guerre de Sécession et l'invention du Canada (2014)

Blood and Daring: How Canada Fought the American Civil War and Forged a Nation (2013)

Bennett: The Rebel Who Challenged and Changed a Nation (2010)

Into the Hurricane: Attacking Socialism and the CCF (2006)

Last Steps to Freedom: The Evolution of Canadian Racism (1995)

Politics: Conflict and Compromise (1990)